CASSEROLES

by
Jean Paré

Cover Photo

1. Sweet and Sour Sausages page 85
2. Curried Rice page 32

CASSEROLES

Twenty-second Edition November, 1989

I.S.B.N. 0-9690695-1-0

Published and Distributed by
Company's Coming Publishing Limited
Box 8037, Station "F"
Edmonton, Alberta, Canada
T6H 4N9

Printed in Canada

Cookbooks in the Company's Coming series by Jean Paré:

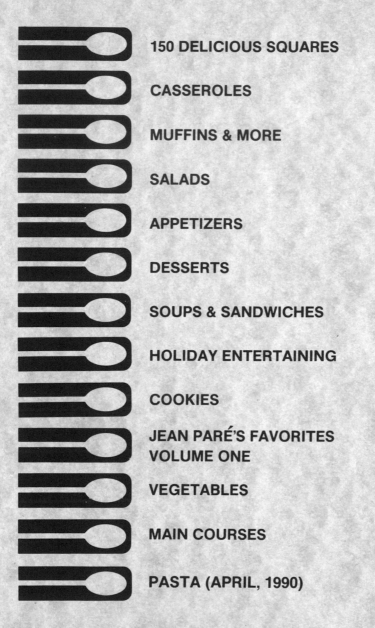

150 DELICIOUS SQUARES

CASSEROLES

MUFFINS & MORE

SALADS

APPETIZERS

DESSERTS

SOUPS & SANDWICHES

HOLIDAY ENTERTAINING

COOKIES

JEAN PARÉ'S FAVORITES VOLUME ONE

VEGETABLES

MAIN COURSES

PASTA (APRIL, 1990)

table of Contents

the Jean Paré story

Jean Paré was born and raised during the Great Depression in Irma, a small farm town in eastern Alberta. She grew up understanding that the combination of family, friends and home cooking is the essence of a good life. Jean learned from her mother, Ruby Elford, to appreciate good cooking and was encouraged by her father, Edward Elford, who praised even her earliest attempts. When she left home she took with her many acquired family recipes, her love of cooking and her intriguing desire to read recipe books like novels!

While raising a family of four, Jean was always busy in her kitchen preparing delicious, tasty treats and savory meals for family and friends of all ages. Her reputation flourished as the mom who would happily feed the neighborhood.

In 1963, when her children had all reached school age, Jean volunteered to cater to the 50th anniversary of the Vermilion School of Agriculture, now Lakeland College. Working out of her home, Jean prepared a dinner for over 1000 people which launched a flourishing catering operation that continued for over eighteen years. During that time she was provided with countless opportunities to test new ideas with immediate feedback —resulting in empty plates and contented customers! Whether preparing cocktail sandwiches for a house party or serving a hot meal for 1500 people, Jean Paré earned a reputation for good food, courteous service and reasonable prices.

"Why don't you write a cookbook?" Time and again Jean was asked that question as requests for her recipes mounted. Jean's response was to team up with her son Grant Lovig in the fall of 1980 to form Company's Coming Publishing Limited. April 14, 1981 marked the debut of "150 DELICIOUS SQUARES", the first Company's Coming cookbook in what soon would become Canada's most popular cookbook series. Jean released a new title each year for the first six years. The pace quickened and by 1987 the company had begun publishing two titles each year.

Jean Paré's operation has grown from the early days of working out of a spare bedroom in her home to operating a large and fully equipped test kitchen in Vermilion, near the home she and her husband Larry built. Full time staff has grown steadily to include marketing personnel located in major cities across Canada. Home Office is located in Edmonton, Alberta where distribution, accounting and administration functions are headquartered. Company's Coming cookbooks are now distributed throughout Canada and the United States plus numerous overseas markets.

Jean Paré's approach to cooking has always called for easy-to-follow recipes using mostly common, affordable ingredients. Her wonderful collection of time-honored recipes, many of which are family heirlooms, are a welcome addition to any kitchen. That's why we say: taste the tradition.

To my family who prompted me to write my first book,
and to my readers who demanded that I write my second.

Foreword

Casseroles are fast becoming a favorite choice among people of all walks of life. Ever tightening schedules for homemakers and their families have resulted in a need for meals suited to advance preparation.

As a rule, casserole preparation is found to be somewhat less than exacting. You will find that it is possible to slightly change the amount of main ingredients used without jeopardizing the end result.

Every casserole in this book (except for those few noted otherwise) can be prepared in advance and can also be frozen. Be sure to allow up to double the specified time for cooking frozen casseroles.

The number and size of servings are variable, dependent upon your choice of accompaniments. For larger gatherings, some popular easy to increase recipes are also included.

Hamburger can indeed be company fare. This popular and economical meat can easily be transformed into many attractive, tasty casseroles which would do justice to any table setting.

Delicious casseroles can be made by even the most inexperienced cook. The tasty combinations of meats, vegetables, poultry, fish or seafood will have family and friends coming back for more.

So warm up the oven — company's coming for casseroles!

Jean Paré

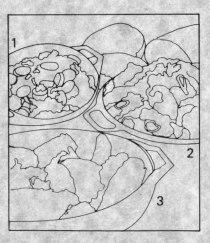

BEV'S CHICKEN CASSEROLE

A real winner. So simple to assemble, it is hard to believe it ends up as a gourmet dish. Although traditionally served with rice the sauce is delicious over mashed potatoes.

Chicken pieces, skin removed	2½-3 lbs.	1.1-1.4 kg
Garlic powder	½-¾ tsp.	3-4 mL
Salt	1 tsp.	5 mL
Pepper	¼ tsp.	1 mL
Condensed tomato soup	10 oz.	284 mL
Condensed cream of mushroom soup	10 oz.	284 mL
Bunch green onions and tops finely cut	1	1
Small onion, chopped	1	1
Fresh tomato, chopped	1	1

Arrange chicken pieces in bottom of large casserole or small roaster. Sprinkle with garlic, salt and pepper.

Combine both soups with onions and tomato. Spoon over chicken. Cover. Bake in 350ºF (180ºC) oven for 2 hours or until tender. Serves 4.

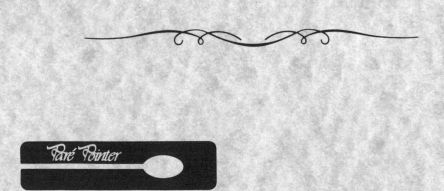

Peanut who walks on lonely street is apt to be assaulted.

CHICKEN HURRY

good

One of the quickest to assemble with no prebrowning.

Chicken parts	2½-3 lbs.	1.1-1.4 kg
Ketchup	½ cup	125 mL
Water	¼ cup	50 mL
Packed brown sugar	¼ cup	50 mL
Envelope dry onion soup mix	1½ oz.	42.5 g

Arrange chicken parts in small roaster or casserole.

In small bowl, combine ketchup, water, sugar and soup mix. Mix together well. Spoon over chicken making sure some is on every piece. Bake covered in 350°F (180°C) oven for at least 1 hour until very tender. Serves 4-6.

Pictured on page 9.

CHICKEN IN CREAM

This scrumptious chicken is turned out in top-of-the-stove fashion.

Chicken parts	2½-3 lbs.	1.2-1.4 kg
Water to cover		
Cream, fairly thick	3-3½ cups	750 mL
Medium onion, sliced	1	1
Salt	1 tsp.	5 mL
Pepper	¼ tsp.	1 mL

Put chicken parts into large saucepan. Cover with water. Boil 1 hour. Drain.

Pour cream over chicken. Add onion, salt and pepper. Bring to boil. Allow to simmer, covered, for 30 minutes or until tender. May be put in casserole and held in warm oven. Serves 4-6.

This is so good you will probably make sure to have leftover turkey.

Broad noodles	6 oz.	170 g
Chopped onion	1½ cups	350 mL
Chopped celery	2 cups	500 mL
Butter or margarine	2 tbsp.	30 mL
Cooked turkey, packed down	4 cups	900 mL
Condensed cream of mushroom soup	10 oz.	284 mL
Condensed cream of chicken soup	10 oz.	284 mL
Sliced mushrooms, drained	10 oz.	284 mL
Salt	1 tsp.	5 mL
Pepper	¼ tsp.	1 mL

Cook noodles according to package directions. Drain.

Put onion, celery and butter in frying pan. Sauté until limp. Add to noodles.

Add turkey, mushroom soup, chicken soup, mushrooms, salt and pepper. Stir. Pour into large casserole. Bake uncovered in 350°F (180°C) oven for 35 minutes until bubbly hot. Serves 6-8.

Paré Pointer

Even lobsters get divorced when they discover they are married to a crab.

HOT CHICKEN SALAD

Turkey works in this casserole too. Just the right tang.

Cooked chicken, chopped	2 cups	500 mL
French dressing	¼ cup	50 mL
Finely chopped celery	½ cup	125 mL
Mayonnaise	½ cup	125 mL
Salt	¼ tsp.	2 mL
Dried onion flakes	1 tsp.	5 mL
Toasted slivered almonds (optional)	2 tbsp.	30 mL
Cheese spread	½ cup	125 mL
French fried onion rings, frozen	4 oz.	113 g

Combine chicken and dressing together in bowl. Put in refrigerator to marinate for 2 hours.

Add celery, mayonnaise, salt and onion flakes to chicken. If you are going to use almonds, toast in 350°F (180°C) oven for 15 minutes. Add to chicken mixture. Pack in 1½-quart (1.5L) casserole.

Put dabs of cheese here and there over chicken. Spread as best you can. Bake uncovered in 350°F (180°C) oven for 35 minutes.

Arrange the onion rings over top and bake 10 minutes more. Serves 4.

Black-eyed peas really don't come from vines that have been fighting.

A colorful top-of-the-stove dish.

Ingredient	Imperial	Metric
Minute rice or regular rice equivalent	2½ cups	500 mL
Water	2½ cups	500 mL
Mushrooms, buttons or sliced	10 oz.	284 mL
Water chestnuts, sliced	10 oz.	284 mL
Celery stalks, sliced thinly on angle	2	2
Chopped green pepper	¼ cup	50 mL
Chopped fresh green onion tops	⅓ cup	75 mL
Chopped pimiento, or strips	2 tbsp.	30 mL
Cut up turkey	1½-2 cups	400 mL
Onion, thinly sliced lengthwise	½ cup	125 mL
Butter or margarine	½ cup	125 mL
Eggs, fork-beaten	3	3
Salt	1½ tsp.	7 mL
Pepper	¼ tsp.	1 mL
Chinese bean sprouts with juice	19 oz.	540 mL
Soy sauce	1 tbsp.	15 mL

Prepare minute rice or cook regular rice. Cool.

In large bowl combine drained mushrooms, drained, sliced water chestnuts, celery, green pepper, green onions, pimiento, turkey and sliced onions. Set aside.

Melt butter in frying pan. Add slightly beaten eggs, salt and pepper. Fry for a few moments, stirring with fork to keep broken up. Do not allow eggs to become too firm. Add rice and meat mixture. Stir to combine over low heat. Add a bit of water to simmer if too dry.

Stir in sprouts and soy sauce. Simmer covered 10-15 minutes till hot. If too dry, add 2 tbsp. (30 mL) butter or margarine. Serves 8.

Pictured on page 81.

SPEEDY CHICKEN

Just two ingredients and as many minutes, finds this in the oven. Use foil for easy cleanup. A favorite.

Chicken parts or cut up chicken	2½-3 lbs.	1.1-1.4 kg
Envelope dry onion soup mix	1½ oz.	42.5 g

Arrange chicken pieces over foil in roaster. Sprinkle evenly with dry onion soup. Fold foil over top. Cover roaster. Bake in 350°F (180°C) oven for 1½-2 hours until tender. Serves 4.

TASTY TURKEY

good

Use either leftover turkey or a can from your shelf. Good eating!

Condensed cream of chicken or cream of mushroom soup	10 oz.	284 mL
Water	¼ cup	50 mL
Chow mein noodles	1 cup	250 mL
Can of turkey (or chicken)	6½ oz.	184 g
Sliced celery	1 cup	250 mL
Chopped onion	⅔ cup	150 mL

Chow mein noodles

Combine soup, water and noodles in 1½-quart (1.5L) casserole. Stir together. Drain turkey. Break up over soup mixture. Toss together.

Add celery and onion. Mix together. Smooth top.

Cover with chow mein noodles. Bake uncovered in 375°F (190°C) oven for 45 minutes. Serves 4.

Delicious! Allow extra time for preparation. Can be made well in advance.

Ham, sliced thin enough to roll

Butter or margarine	4 tbsp.	50 mL
All-purpose flour	3 tbsp.	45 mL
Salt	½ tsp.	3 mL
Pepper	⅛ tsp.	1 mL
Milk	1 cup	250 mL
Cooked chicken or turkey cut in small pieces	1½ cups	375 mL
Finely chopped celery	½ cup	125 mL
Finely chopped green pepper	¼ cup	50 mL
Chopped olives (optional)		
Sliced mushrooms, drained	10 oz.	284 mL
Condensed cream of mushroom soup	10 oz.	284 mL
Milk	⅓ cup	75 mL
White wine (optional)	2 tbsp.	30 mL

Slice ham thin enough to allow for rolling. You will need about 10-12 slices. Set aside in refrigerator.

Melt butter in saucepan. Stir in flour, salt and pepper. Add milk. Cook and stir until it boils and thickens. It will be thick.

Add chicken, celery, green pepper, olives and mushrooms. Mix together well. Divide on ham slices. Roll and secure with toothpick. Arrange in casserole with the pick side up.

In small bowl, mix soup, milk and wine. Pour over ham rolls. Bake uncovered in 350°F (180°C) oven for 40 minutes. Baste often as it cooks. Serves 8-10.

CHICKEN IN GRAVY

Takes time to prepare but, how it is worth it at meal time!

All-purpose flour	⅓ cup	75 mL
Salt	1 tsp.	5 mL
Pepper	¼ tsp.	1 mL
Paprika	1 tsp.	5 mL
Young chicken, cut up or chicken parts	3 lbs.	1.4 kg
Butter or margarine	4 tbsp.	60 mL
All-purpose flour	5 tbsp.	75 mL
Butter or margarine	1-4 tbsp.	15-60 mL
Water	4 cups	900 mL
Salt	1 tsp.	5 mL
Pepper	¼ tsp.	1 mL

Put flour, salt, pepper and paprika in paper or plastic bag. Shake to mix.

Put in damp chicken pieces 3 at a time. Shake to coat.

Put into heated butter in frying pan. Brown both sides. Transfer to small casserole or small roaster.

GRAVY

Stir flour into fat in pan, adding butter to mix if needed. Add water stirring until boiling. Should be fairly thin. It will thicken in roaster. Pour over chicken. Cover. Bake in 350°F (180°C) oven for 1 hour or until fork tender. Taste and add salt if needed.

Also good if gravy is omitted. Serves 4.

CHICKEN AND PORK ADOBO

These are the two favorite meats of the Philippines served up in a dish fit for all visitors. Served with rice.

Ingredient	Imperial	Metric
Vinegar	½ cup	125 mL
Garlic powder (or 1 clove minced)	¼ tsp.	1 mL
Salt	2 tsp.	10 mL
Pepper	½ tsp.	2 mL
Soy sauce	2 tbsp.	30 mL
Water	2 cups	500 mL
Paprika	½ tsp.	2 mL
Lean pork cut up	1 lb.	500 g
Chicken meat cut up	2 lbs.	1 kg

In 2-quart (2L) casserole put vinegar, garlic, salt, pepper, soy sauce, water and paprika, Stir.

Cut up pork and chicken. Put in casserole. Cover. Bake in 350°F (180°C) oven for 1 ½ hours or until tender. Serves 6.

QUICK SOUFFLÉ

Anyone can make this. Similar in taste to a puffy omelet.

Ingredient	Imperial	Metric
Condensed cream of chicken soup (or mushroom or asparagus)	10 oz.	284 mL
Egg yolks	4	4
Egg whites	4	4

In medium-sized bowl put soup and egg yolks. Mix together well.

Beat egg whites until stiff. Fold into soup mixture. Pile into greased 1-quart (1L) casserole. Bake in 425°F (220°C) oven for 25 minutes. Serve immediately.

CHICKEN SUPREME

To add flair to a special meal try this easy to make casserole.

All-purpose flour	⅓ cup	75 mL
Salt	1 tsp.	5 mL
Pepper	¼ tsp.	1 mL
Paprika	1 tsp.	5 mL
Chicken Parts	2½-3 lbs.	1.1-1.4 kg
Butter or margarine	4 tbsp.	60 mL
Condensed cream of mushroom soup	10 oz.	284 mL
Sliced mushrooms, drained	10 oz.	284 mL
White wine (or apple juice)	¼ cup	50 mL
Medium carrot cut in thin strips	1	1

Combine flour, salt, pepper and paprika together in paper bag. Shake to mix well.

Add damp chicken parts, 3 at a time. Shake to coat.

Melt butter in frying pan. Add chicken. Brown well. Transfer to casserole or small roaster.

Empty soup into medium-sized bowl. Add drained mushrooms and wine. Stir well. Pour over chicken. Cover. Bake in 350°F (180°C) oven for 1 hour.

Peel carrot. Cut into 2 or 3-inch (5-7 cm) lengths. Cut into very thin strips. Add to chicken. Continue to cook covered for 15 minutes or until chicken is tender. Serve with brown rice.
Serves 4.

CHICKEN CACCIATORE

Traditionally served over spaghetti but good any other way too.

Cooking oil	4 tbsp.	50 mL
Chicken parts	2½ lbs.	1 kg
Garlic clove, minced	1	1
Chopped onion	½ cup	125 mL
Spaghetti sauce	1¾ cup	450 mL
Parsley	1 tbsp.	15 mL
Sherry or white wine (optional)	¼ cup	50 mL
Salt	½ tsp.	2 mL
Pepper	¼ tsp.	1 mL

Heat oil in frying pan. Add chicken, garlic and onion. Brown well. Put in large casserole or small roaster.

In medium bowl combine spaghetti sauce with parsley, sherry, salt and pepper. Pour over chicken. Bake covered in 350°F (180°C) oven for 1 hour or until tender. Serves 4.

All too often opportunity presents itself disguised as hard work.

CHICKEN POT PIE

There is a delicious meal under that crust.

Cooked chicken, cut up	3 cups	700 mL
Mushroom pieces, drained	10 oz.	284 mL
Sliced carrots, cooked	2 cups	450 mL
Cooked potatoes, cut up	2 cups	450 mL
Frozen peas, cooked	1 cup	250 mL
Onions, chopped and cooked	½ cup	125 mL
Leftover gravy	2 cups	500 mL
Chicken bouillon cubes	2	2
Onion powder	¼ tsp.	1 mL
Celery salt	¼ tsp.	1 mL

Pastry for top — your own or a mix. See page 127.

Put chicken and mushroom pieces into 3-quart (4L) casserole. Add cooked vegetables. Be sure to cook vegetables in salted water. Stir lightly.

Heat gravy. Add bouillon cubes. Crush and stir to dissolve. Stir in onion powder and celery salt. Pour over meat and vegetables lifting with fork here and there to let gravy run through. Have gravy not too thick.

Roll out pastry to fit circle ½ inch (2 cm) larger in diameter than casserole top. Put over top with pastry fitting up sides a bit. Cut slits in pastry. Bake in 400°F (200°C) oven for 30 minutes or until heated through and light brown. Serves 6.

GRAVY
If you have no gravy, this is a good substitute. It is salty so do not add salt to vegetable cooking water. With the meat and vegetables to absorb the salt, it will be just right.

Chicken bouillon cubes	6	6
Beef bouillon cube	1	1
Water	2 cups	450 mL

(continued on next page)

Celery Salt	½ tsp.	2 mL
Onion powder	½ tsp.	2 mL
Cornstarch	2 tbsp.	30 mL
Water	½ cup	125 mL

Put bouillon cubes and water in medium-sized saucepan. Stir to dissolve as you bring to boil.

Add celery salt and onion powder.

Mix cornstarch and water together. Pour into boiling juice stirring until it boils again. Proceed as above.

TURKEY PIE

A regular feature after a turkey dinner.

Cooked turkey, cut up	2 cups	450 mL
Condensed cream of mushroom soup	10 oz.	284 mL
Chopped celery, cooked	1 cup	225 mL
Milk	¾ cup	175 mL
Salt	½ tsp.	2 mL
Pepper	⅛ tsp.	0.5 mL
Packaged biscuit mix	2 cups	450 mL
Milk, as directed on package	¾ cup	175 mL

Put turkey, soup and cooked celery in 1½-quart (1.5L) casserole. Stir in milk, salt and pepper. Heat in 400°F (200°C) oven until bubbling hot.

Mix biscuit mix and milk as for dumplings. Drop by spoonful over top of hot meat and sauce. Bake in 450°F (230°C) oven for 15 minutes or until brown. Serves 4-6.

SEAFOOD SUPREME

An extra special treat when cost is no object.

Canned lobster	5 oz.	142 g
Canned shrimp	4 oz.	113 g
Canned crab	5 oz.	142 g
Canned chicken	6½ oz.	184 g
Scallops, fresh or frozen	½ lb.	250 g
Butter or margarine	½ cup	125 mL
All-purpose flour	½ cup	125 mL
Dry mustard	¼ tsp.	1 mL
Salt	½ tsp.	2 mL
Milk	2 cups	450 mL
Sour cream	1 cup	250 mL
Sherry or white wine (or apple juice)	½ cup	125 mL
Butter or margarine for topping	2 tbsp.	30 mL
Bread crumbs	1 cup	250 mL
Grated cheese	½ cup	125 mL

Put lobster, shrimp, crab and chicken into large bowl. Break into bite-sized pieces, removing membrane.

Cover scallops with water in medium saucepan. Boil 5 minutes. Drain. Cut in half and add to bowl. Set aside.

In same saucepan, melt butter. Stir in flour, mustard and salt. Add milk. Cook, stirring, until mixture boils.

Add sour cream and sherry or wine. Pour over contents in bowl. Stir lightly to combine. Pour into 2½-quart (3L) casserole.

Melt butter in saucepan. Remove from heat. Stir in crumbs to coat. Add cheese. Stir lightly. Spread over top of casserole. Bake at 350° F (180° C) oven for 20-30 minutes until hot and bubbly. Serves 12.

Pictured on page 27.

Good as the only main dish or as an extra.

Eggs	2	2
Lemon juice	3 tbsp.	50 mL
Instant onion flakes (optional)	1 tsp.	5 mL
Butter or margarine	1 tbsp.	15 mL
Salt	1 tsp.	5 mL
Pepper	¼ tsp.	1 mL
Salmon	2 — 7¾ oz.	2 — 220 g
Milk	¾ cup	175 mL
Bread crumbs	2 cups	450 mL

chopped green onion + cellery

Beat eggs until frothy. Add lemon juice and beat again. Add onion, butter, salt and pepper. Mix well.

Remove skin and round bones from salmon. Mash with juice. Add to egg mixture.

Add milk and crumbs. Mix well. Pack into 1½-quart (1.5L) greased casserole. Bake in 350°F (180°C) oven for 1 hour. Serves 6.

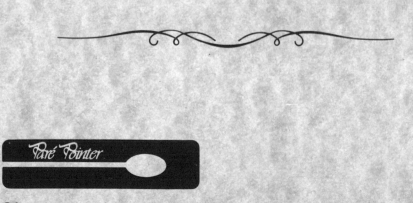

Paré Pointer

Of course you know that little baby chickens dance chick to chick.

SALMON BALL CASSEROLE

This is one of the most appetizing ways of serving salmon. Make the balls smaller if using as a second meat. Pink salmon works fine. Use red if you want more color.

Tinned salmon	2 — 7¾ oz.	2 — 220 g
Long-grain rice, raw	½ cup	125 mL
Grated carrot	½ cup	125 mL
Chopped onion	¼ cup	50 mL
Egg	1	1
Salt	½ tsp.	2 mL
Pepper	⅛ tsp.	0.5 mL
Condensed cream of mushroom soup	10 oz.	284 mL
Water	½ cup	125 mL

Put salmon and juice into medium-sized bowl. Remove skin and round bones.

Add rice, carrot, onion, egg, salt and pepper. Mix together well. Shape into balls and put in casserole leaving room for expansion. Sixteen balls are just right for 9 x 9-inch (23 x 23 cm) dish.

Mix soup and water together. Pour over top. Bake covered in oven at 350°F (180°C) for about 1 hour. Serves 5-6.

Pictured on page 27.

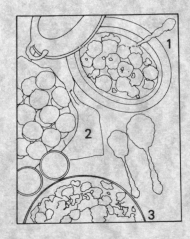

1. Salmon Ball Casserole page 26
2. Baking Powder Biscuits page 126
3. Seafood Supreme page 24

For a special party and special company. Quick to prepare.

Butter or margarine	½ cup	125 mL
All-purpose flour	¾ cup	175 mL
Salt	2 tsp.	10 mL
Milk	4 cups	900 mL
Tomato paste	3 tbsp.	45 mL
Lemon juice	1 tbsp.	15 mL
Worcestershire sauce	2 tsp.	10 mL
Butter or margarine	2 tbsp.	30 mL
Button mushrooms, drained	2 — 10 oz.	2 — 284 mL
Scallops	1 lb.	500 g
Lobster	2 — 5 oz.	2 — 142 g
Medium-sized shrimp	2 — 4 oz.	2 — 113 g

In large saucepan melt ½ cup (125 mL) butter. Stir in flour and salt. Add milk. Stir and cook until mixture boils and thickens.

Add tomato paste, lemon juice and Worcestershire sauce. Remove from heat and set aside.

Melt 2 tbsp. (30 mL) butter in frying pan. Add mushrooms and sauté until golden brown. Stir into sauce.

In medium saucepan, combine scallops with enough water to cover. Bring to boil. Simmer 5 minutes. Drain. Cut large scallops in half. Add to sauce.

Drain lobster and shrimp. Break lobster into bite-sized pieces, removing any cartilage. Add lobster and shrimp into sauce. Heat over low heat or transfer to casserole to be heated when needed. Heat covered in 350°F (180°C) oven for 30 minutes until hot. Serves 12-14.

CRAB DELUXE

A real treat. Great for luncheons.

Condensed cream of mushroom soup	10 oz.	284 mL
Water	¼ cup	50 mL
Chow mein noodles	1 cup	250 mL
Can of crab	4¾ oz.	135 g
Sliced celery	1 cup	225 mL
Chopped onion	1 cup	225 mL
Parsley flakes	2 tsp.	10 mL

Chow mein noodles

Stir soup, water and noodles together in a 1½-quart (1.5L) casserole.

Drain crab. Break up large pieces removing any cartilage. Add to soup mixture.

Add celery, onion and parsley. Stir together lightly. Smooth top.

Cover top with dry noodles. Bake uncovered in 375°F (190°C) oven for 45 minutes or microwave on high power 9 minutes. Serves 4.

 Paré Pointer

You're in trouble at a football game if you think a quarterback is a refund.

SEAFOOD CASSEROLE

Fit for your best entertaining. Takes extra time.

Butter or margarine	¼ cup	60 mL
All-purpose flour	¼ cup	60 mL
Salt	1 tsp.	5 mL
Dash of cayenne		
Milk	2 cups	450 mL
Worcestershire sauce	1 tsp.	5 mL
Grated Cheddar cheese	½ cup	125 mL
Instant onion flakes	1 tsp.	5 mL
Scallops	2 cups	500 mL
Lobster or crab meat, diced	1½ cups	350 mL
Minced parsley	1 tbsp.	15 mL
Butter or margarine for topping	2 tbsp.	30 mL
Bread crumbs	1 cup	250 mL

Melt butter in medium saucepan. Stir in flour, salt and cayenne.

Add milk. Stir and bring to boil. Remove from heat.

Add Worcestershire sauce, cheese and onion. Stir to melt cheese.

In medium saucepan, cover scallops with water. Bring to boil. Boil 5 minutes. Drain. Cut large scallops in half. Add to sauce.

Add lobster or crab removing any cartilage. Add parsley. Stir together. Spoon into individual shells or large casserole.

In small saucepan melt butter. Stir in crumbs. Cover shells or casserole with buttered crumbs. Heat in 350°F (180°C) oven until bubbly. Serves 6.

CURRIED RICE

Makes a great extra. Nice aroma. Looks pretty. Really good.

Minute rice	2 cups	450 mL
Butter or margarine	1 tbsp.	15 mL
All-purpose flour	1 tbsp.	15 mL
Milk	1½ cups	350 mL
Salad dressing	½ cup	125 mL
Curry powder	½ tsp.	2 mL
Chopped pimiento	2 tbsp.	30 mL
Instant onion flakes	1 tbsp.	15 mL
Shrimp, small size, drained	4 oz.	113 g

Prepare rice as directed on package. Put into shallow baking dish. Keep warm.

In medium saucepan, melt butter. Stir in flour. Add milk. Bring to boil, stirring. Will be fairly thin.

Add salad dressing, curry, pimiento and onion.

Drain shrimp. Stir shrimp into sauce. Mix and pour evenly over rice. Stir fork here and there to allow some sauce to penetrate. Ready to serve. Or cover and put in warm oven to hold. Serves 12 as an extra. Add extra ¼ cup (50 mL) milk if held in oven.

Pictured on cover.

Paré Pointer

About the least you can buy for your girl is a bikini.

A classic! Suitable for a chafing dish.

Butter or margarine	6 tbsp.	100 mL
All-purpose flour	2 tbsp.	30 mL
Salt	¼ tsp.	1 mL
Light cream	1 cup	250 mL
Egg yolks, fork beaten	3	3
Lobster	5 oz.	142 g
Brandy	1 tbsp.	15 mL
Sherry	1 tbsp.	15 mL
Lemon juice	1 tsp.	5 mL
Paprika	⅛ tsp.	0.5 mL

In top of double broiler melt butter. Put over direct heat. Stir in flour and salt. Add cream stirring until boiling. Put egg yolks in small dish. Add some hot mixture to yolks. Stir. Empty yolk mixture into sauce stirring briskly. Put saucepan over hot water.

Break lobster into bite-sized pieces, removing any cartilage. Add to sauce. Heat through.

Stir in brandy, sherry, lemon juice and paprika. Serve in patty shells or toast cups. Serves 4-5.

Paré Pointer

Educate a man without religion and you end up with a clever devil.

CRAB QUICHE

This does double duty as a main dish or as an appetizer. It has a very creamy filling.

Eggs	3	3
Sour cream	¾ cup	175 mL
Milk	½ cup	125 mL
Salt	½ tsp.	2 mL
Dry mustard	¼ tsp.	2 mL
Cayenne	dash	dash
Crabmeat	5 oz.	142 g
Grated Swiss cheese	1 cup	225 mL
(or 4 slices cut up small)		
Chives	2 tbsp.	30 mL
Lemon juice	1 tbsp.	15 mL
Unbaked pastry-lined quiche dish — see page 127	9 inch	23 cm

In mixing bowl beat eggs until frothy. Add sour cream, milk, salt, mustard and cayenne. Beat to blend.

Drain crabmeat. Break up, removing cartilage. Add to egg mixture. Add cheese, chives and lemon juice. Stir to mix.

Pour into uncooked pie shell. Bake in 425°F (220°C) oven for 15 minutes on lower shelf. Turn heat to 350°F (180°C). Bake 30-40 minutes longer until a knife inserted near center comes out clean. Cut into 6 wedges to serve as a main dish, or 12 as an appetizer.

For a touch of color and spice, add 1 tbsp. (15 mL) ketchup.

Paré Pointer

A sleeping bull is better known as a bulldozer.

T̶h̶e̶ ... vor comes through in this wholesome meal-in-one dish.

Macaroni, raw	¾ cup	175 mL
Condensed cream of celery soup	10 oz.	284 mL
Milk	⅓ cup	75 mL
Peas, frozen or fresh	1½ cups	350 mL
Cheese slices, broken up	4	4
Salt	½ tsp.	2 mL
Dash of pepper		
Tuna	7 oz.	198 g
Cheese slices for top	2	2

Cook macaroni as directed on package. Rinse with cold water. Drain. Pour into greased 1½-quart (1.5L) casserole. Set aside.

In medium-sized saucepan combine soup, milk, peas and cheese slices. Heat and stir until hot and cheese is melted. Add salt and pepper to taste. Pour over macaroni.

Drain tuna. Break up into pieces and put on top of sauce. Stir lightly to combine all together. Cover. Bake in 350°F (180°C) oven for 20 minutes.

Remove cover. Cut cheese slices diagonally to make 4 triangles. Arrange over casserole. Bake uncovered 5 minutes or until cheese is melted. Serves 4.

TUNA LASAGNE

Good for any meal, especially luncheons. Real tasty.

Lasagne noodles	8 oz.	225 g
Butter or margarine	2 tbsp.	30 mL
Medium onion, chopped	1	1
Garlic powder (or 1 garlic clove minced)	¼ tsp.	1 mL
All-purpose flour	2 tbsp.	30 mL
Condensed cream of celery soup	10 oz.	284 mL
Milk	½ cup	125 mL
Dried chives	1 tsp.	5 mL
Oregano	¼ tsp.	1 mL
Pepper	⅛ tsp.	0.5 mL
Tuna	6½ oz.	184 g
Large tomato, sliced	1	1
Swiss or Cheddar cheese slices	4	4

Cook noodles as directed on package. Rinse with cold water. Drain.

SAUCE

Put butter in frying pan. Add onion and garlic. Sauté slowly until limp.

Sprinkle with flour and stir.

Add soup, milk, chives, oregano, pepper and tuna to onions. Stir to blend.

(continued on next page)

Assemble as follows in 8 x 8-inch (20 x 20) pan.

1. A bit of sauce on bottom
2. ⅓ noodles
3. ⅓ sauce
4. ⅓ noodles
5. ⅓ sauce
6. ⅓ noodles
7. ⅓ sauce
8. Arrange tomato slices over sauce
9. Put on cheese slices

Bake uncovered in 350°F (180°C) oven for 20-30 minutes. Serves 4.

To Freeze — Add ½ tsp. (2 mL) salt to sauce. Omit steps 8 and 9. Cover tightly and freeze.

To Serve — Bake covered in 450°F (230°C) oven for 1 hour. Uncover. Do steps 8 and 9. Bake uncovered 350°F (180°C) oven for 20 minutes.

TUNA CASSEROLE

Just right for a planned or a spur-of-the-moment meal. Can be doubled easily.

Condensed cream of mushroom soup	10 oz.	284 mL
Water	¼ cup	50 mL
Chow mein noodles	1 cup	250 mL
Tuna	7 oz.	198 g
Sliced celery	1 cup	250 mL
Chopped onion	1 cup	250 mL
Chow mein noodles		

In 1½-quart (1.5L) casserole, put soup, water and first amount of noodles. Toss together.

Drain tuna and add along with sliced celery and onion. Mix together lightly.

Cover top with extra noodles. Bake uncovered in 375° F (190° C) oven for 45 minutes or microwave on high power for 9 minutes. Serves 4.

To make this super special, add 1 cup (225 mL) salted, toasted cashew nuts to casserole ingredients.

Should robots ever be buried, a suitable epitaph would read "Rust in peace".

Quick to assemble and really flavorful. A great zesty "take to the lake" dish.

Ground beef	2 lbs.	1 kg
Onion, chopped	1 medium	1 medium
Cooking oil	¼ cup	50 mL
Kernel corn	12 oz.	341 mL
Condensed tomato soup	2 − 10 oz.	2 − 284 mL
Salt	1 tsp.	5 mL
Pepper	½ tsp.	2 mL
Ketchup	1 tbsp.	15 mL
Cooked noodles	2 cups	500 mL
Grated Cheddar cheese	1 cup	250 mL

Put ground beef, onion and oil into frying pan. Stir to break up meat as it browns. Drain off fat. Discard. Put meat mixture into large bowl.

Put corn, soup, salt, pepper and ketchup into same bowl. Stir to mix together with meat.

Prepare noodles according to package directions. Drain. Measure. Combine with all ingredients in bowl. Pour into 3-quart (3.5L) casserole.

Sprinkle grated cheese over top. Cover. Bake in 350ºF (180ºC) oven for 45 minutes. Remove cover and continue to bake until cheese is melted and bubbly. Serves 6-8.

MUNCHIN' LUNCHEON

The green pepper perks this up just the right amount. A showy dish with the red showing beneath the crumb topping.

Kernel corn	1 cup	250 mL
Cooking oil	¼ cup	50 mL
Chopped onion	1 cup	250 mL
Green pepper, chopped	1	1
Ground beef	1 lb.	500 g
Salt	1 tsp.	5 mL
Pepper	¼ tsp.	1 mL
Canned tomatoes	14 oz.	398 mL
Minute tapioca	1 tbsp.	15 mL
Butter or margarine	1 tbsp.	15 mL
Dry breadcrumbs	½ cup	125 mL

Spread corn over bottom of 1½-quart (1.5L) casserole.

Put oil in frying pan. Add onion, green pepper, ground beef, salt and pepper. Fry, stirring to break up, until browned. Drain off fat and discard. Spread mixture over corn.

Stir tomatoes and tapioca together. Pour evenly over meat layer.

In small saucepan, melt butter. Add crumbs, stirring to coat evenly. Sprinkle over top. Bake uncovered in 350ºF (180ºC) oven for 35 minutes. Serves 4.

BEEFY DAIRY CASSEROLE

A great surprise awaits you when you try this dish. It is just so mellow!

Ground beef	1 lb.	500 g
Chopped onion	½ cup	125 mL
Cooking oil	1 tbsp.	15 mL
Milk	½ cup	125 mL
Cream cheese	8 oz.	250 g
Condensed cream of mushroom soup	10 oz.	284 mL
Kernel corn	12 oz.	341 mL
Chopped pimiento	¼ cup	50 mL
Cooked noodles	2 cups	500 mL
Salt	1½ tsp.	7 mL
Pepper	¼ tsp.	1 mL

Put beef, onion and oil in frying pan. Scramble fry until meat is browned. Drain off any fat. Spoon meat into 2-quart (2.5L) casserole. Set aside.

Combine milk with cheese in medium-sized bowl. Mash together with fork.

Add soup, corn, pimiento, noodles, salt and pepper to milk and cheese mixture. Pour all into casserole, stirring to distribute through meat. Bake in 350°F (180°C) oven for 40 minutes. Allow at least an extra 15 minutes if taken from refrigerator to oven. Serves 4.

CURRIED HASH

A touch of the exotic. Curry is middle of the road, use less or more to your liking. Versatile. Makes a good meat sauce.

Cooking oil	1 tbsp.	15 mL
Ground beef	1 ¼ lbs.	620 g
Chopped onion	¾ cup	175 mL
Salt	1 tsp.	5 mL
Pepper	½ tsp.	1 mL
Sage	½ tsp.	2 mL
All-purpose flour	3 tbsp.	45 mL
Milk	2 cups	500 mL
Curry powder	1 tsp.	5 mL

Combine oil, ground beef and onion in frying pan. Brown, stirring frequently to break up. Sprinkle with salt, pepper and sage.

Stir in flour until well mixed with meat mixture. Add milk all at once. Stir as it boils and thickens. Stir in curry powder. Add more liquid if needed, especially when reheating. Ready to eat or put in casserole. Cover. Bake in 350ºF (180ºC) oven for 20 minutes. Serve with rice or oodles of noodles. Serves 4.

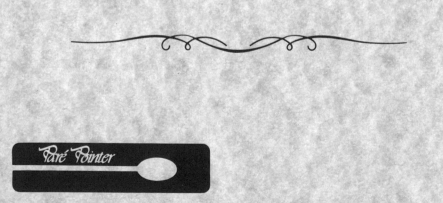

Paré Pointer

If your father is a doctor you can be sick for nothing. If your father is a minister you can be good for nothing.

HAMBURGER CASSEROLE

A hint of lasagne flavor, milder and tasty.

Cooked small egg noodles	2 cups	500 mL
Ground beef	1 lb.	500 g
Cooking oil	1 tbsp.	15 mL
Chopped onion	1 cup	250 mL
Garlic powder (or minced garlic clove)	¼ tsp.	1 mL
Tomato sauce	2 — 7½ oz.	2 — 213 mL
Salt	1 tsp.	5 mL
Pepper	½ tsp.	2 mL
Sour cream	1 cup	250 mL
Cottage cheese	1 cup	250 mL
Shredded mozzarella cheese	1 cup	250 mL

Prepare noodles as directed on package. Drain. Measure. Spread in bottom of 1½-quart (1.5L) casserole.

Scramble fry beef in oil until brown. Drain and discard fat.

Add onion, garlic, tomato sauce, salt and pepper to meat. Simmer gently for 15 minutes. Pour over noodles in casserole.

Spread sour cream over meat, smoothing level.

Spoon cottage cheese over top.

Layer cheese over top to cover completely. Bake uncovered in 350°F (180°C) oven for 30 minutes until bubbly. Serves 6-8.

CHOP SUEY

To round out your Chinese food menu.

Cooking oil	2 tbsp.	30 mL
Finely chopped celery	¾ cup	175 mL
Finely chopped onion	½ cup	125 mL
Ground beef	1 lb.	500 g
Bean sprouts with juice	19 oz.	540 mL
Mushroom pieces with juice	10 oz.	284 mL
Soy sauce	1 tbsp.	15 mL
Sugar	1 tsp.	5 mL
Salt	½ tsp.	2 mL
Cornstarch	1 tbsp.	15 mL
Water	1 tbsp.	15 mL

Put oil, celery, onion and meat in frying pan. Sauté slowly until meat is browned and vegetables are limp. Set aside.

Empty bean sprouts and mushrooms into large saucepan. Stir in soy sauce, sugar and salt. Bring to boil.

Stir cornstarch and water together in small cup. Pour into boiling mixture stirring until boiling again. Add meat mixture. Ready to serve or hold in casserole. Serves 4.

1. Beef Marguerite page 102
2. Ham Asparagus Rolls page 71
3. Mustard Beans page 128

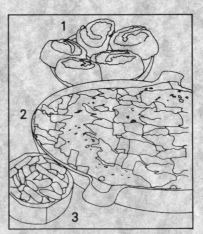

The flavor of corn comes through well. Really simple to assemble.

Ground beef	1½ lbs.	750 g
Chopped onion	1 cup	250 mL
Cooking oil	1 tbsp.	15 mL
Kernel corn, drained	12 oz.	341 mL
Condensed cream of chicken soup	10 oz.	284 mL
Condensed cream of mushroom soup	10 oz.	284 mL
Chopped pimiento or red pepper	¼ cup	50 mL
Sour cream	1 cup	225 mL
Cooked noodles	3 cups	675 mL
Salt	¾ tsp.	4 mL
Monosodium glutamate	½ tsp.	2 mL
Pepper	¼ tsp.	1 mL
Beef in a mug soup powder	1 tsp.	5 mL
Butter or margarine	¼ cup	50 mL
Cornflake crumbs	1 cup	250 mL

Scramble fry ground beef with onions in the oil. Drain off fat. Discard. Remove from heat

Stir in corn, chicken and mushroom soup. Add chopped pimiento and sour cream. Mix lightly. Add prepared drained noodles. Sprinkle salt, monosodium glutamate, pepper and beef powder over top and stir to combine. Pour into 2½-quart (2.5L) casserole.

In small saucepan melt butter. Add cornflake crumbs. Stir to moisten evenly. Spread over top of casserole. Bake uncovered in 350ºF (180ºC) oven for 35-45 minutes until hot. Serves 10.

HAMBURGER ITALIANO

Colorful and good as well. All ingredients manage to show through the top.

Cooking oil	2 tbsp.	30 mL
Ground beef	1 lb.	500 g
Chopped green pepper	⅓ cup	75 mL
Chopped onion	½ cup	125 mL
Chopped celery	¼ cup	50 mL
Canned tomatoes	14 oz.	398 mL
Condensed tomato soup	10 oz.	284 mL
Kernel corn	12 oz.	341 mL
Garlic powder	¼ tsp.	1 mL
Oregano	¼ tsp.	1 mL
Salt	1 tsp.	5 mL
Pepper	¼ tsp.	1 mL
Shredded medium Cheddar cheese	1 cup	250 mL

Combine oil, ground beef, green pepper, onion and celery in frying pan. Fry until all pink color is gone. Stir to break up meat. Drain and discard fat.

Stir tomatoes and soup into meat. Add corn, garlic, oregano, salt and pepper. Simmer slowly for 15 minutes.

Add cheese. Stir to distribute through meat. Pour into 2-quart (2L) casserole. Bake uncovered in 350°F (180°C) oven for 30 minutes until hot and bubbly. Serves 6.

Paré Pointer

The worst thing about being a mud thrower is ground lost.

GOOD TIME CASSEROLE

This is definitely meant for a good time. What a time saver to put this meat and cheese meal from refrigerator to oven to table!

Cooked noodles	4 cups	1 L
Ground beef	2 lbs.	1 kg
Tomato sauce	4 — 7½ oz.	4 — 213 mL
Salt	1 tsp.	5 mL
Pepper	¼ tsp.	1 mL
Garlic salt	1 tsp.	1 mL
Sugar	2 tsp.	10 mL
Cream cheese, softened	8 oz.	250 g
Sour cream	2 cups	500 mL
Green onions, sliced including tops	5	5
Grated medium Cheddar cheese	2 cups	500 mL

Prepare noodles as directed on package. Drain. Measure. Spread in bottom of 4-quart (5L) casserole.

Brown beef in frying pan, stirring to break up chunks. Drain and discard fat.

Add tomato sauce to meat. Measure in salt, pepper, garlic salt and sugar. Stir. Bring to boil. Simmer gently 15 minutes. Spoon over noodles.

In medium-sized bowl, mash cream cheese and sour cream. Stir in green onions. Spread over meat layer.

Sprinkle cheese over top. Bake uncovered in 350°F (180°C) oven for 35 minutes until hot. If cheese begins to dry before casserole is hot enough, cover with lid or foil. Serves 8.

HAMBURGER DELUXE

Deluxe to look at with mushrooms showing on top. Super deluxe to eat.

Cooked noodles	2 cups	500 mL
Cooking oil	2 tbsp.	30 mL
Ground beef	1 lb.	500 g
Green pepper, chopped	1	1
Chopped onion	1 cup	250 mL
Canned mushrooms sliced and drained	⅓ cup	75 mL
Condensed tomato soup	10 oz.	284 mL
Water	1 cup	250 mL
Salt	½ tsp.	2 mL
Paprika	½ tsp.	2 mL
Grated Parmesan cheese	¼ cup	50 mL
Worcestershire sauce	1 tsp.	5 mL

Boil noodles as directed on package. Drain. Measure. Spread over bottom of 2-quart (2L) casserole.

Pour oil in frying pan. Add beef, green pepper and onion. Fry and stir until brown. Drain off fat. Spread meat mixture over noodles.

In medium-sized bowl, combine mushrooms with soup and water. Mix until blended. Add salt, paprika, cheese and Worcestershire sauce. Pour over meat. Bake uncovered in 350°F (180°C) oven for 35-45 minutes. Serves 5-6.

An oriental touch, yet not too! Simple to double.

Cooking oil	2 tbsp.	30 mL
Ground beef	1 lb.	500 g
Green pepper, chopped	1	1
Chopped celery	2 cups	500 mL
Chopped onion	½ cup	125 mL
Sliced mushrooms	10 oz.	284 mL
Milk	¼ cup	50 mL
Condensed cream of mushroom soup	10 oz.	284 mL
Soy sauce	1 tbsp.	15 mL
Salt	1 tsp.	5 mL
Pepper	¼ tsp.	2 mL
Parsley flakes	1 tsp.	5 mL
Butter or margarine	3 tbsp.	50 mL
Chopped almonds	⅓ cup	75 mL
Bread crumbs	1 cup	250 mL

In large frying pan, put oil, beef, green pepper, celery and onions. Scramble fry until meat is brown.

Drain mushrooms. Mix into meat mixture. Stir in milk and soup. Add soy sauce, salt, pepper and parsley flakes. Mix together well and pour into 1½-quart (1.5L) casserole.

Melt butter in small saucepan. Add nuts and crumbs. Stir to coat. Sprinkle over top. Bake uncovered in 350°F (180°C) oven for 40-50 minutes. Serves 5-6.

CHINA BOY HASH

An oriental meal in one, with no precooking of rice.

Cooking oil	2 tbsp.	30 mL
Green pepper, chopped	1	1
Chopped celery	½ cup	125 mL
Chopped onion	1 cup	250 mL
Ground beef	1 lb.	500 g
Boiling water	1 cup	250 mL
Beef bouillon cubes	3	3
Sliced mushrooms, drained	10 oz.	284 mL
Long grain rice	½ cup	125 mL
Water chestnuts, drained and sliced	10 oz.	284 mL
Bamboo shoots	10 oz.	284 mL
Bean sprouts, fresh is best	2 cups	500 mL
Soy sauce	3 tbsp.	50 mL
Salt	1 tsp.	5 mL
Pepper	¼ tsp.	1 mL

Heat oil in frying pan. Add next 4 ingredients in order given. Sauté to soften. Stir to break up meat and continue cooking until no pink color remains. Turn off heat.

In small bowl or saucepan, dissolve bouillon cubes in boiling water. Pour into meat mixture.

Add mushrooms, rice, water chestnuts, bamboo shoots and bean sprouts. Mix lightly to combine. Add soy sauce, salt and pepper. Stir together well. Scoop into 1½-quart (1.5L) casserole. Cover. Bake in 350°F (180°C) oven for 45 minutes until rice is cooked. Serves 4.

A nice flavorful casserole. It has a reddish brown hue with the carrots and peas adding color contrast.

Ground beef	1 lb.	500 g
All-purpose flour	1 tbsp.	15 mL
Tomato sauce	7½ oz.	213 mL
Ketchup	2 tbsp.	30 mL
Peas, frozen or fresh	1 cup	250 mL
Canned stewed tomatoes	14 oz.	398 mL
Carrots, sliced and cooked	1 cup	250 mL
Water	½ cup	125 mL
Salt	½ tsp.	2 mL

Brown ground beef in frying pan.

Sprinkle flour over beef and stir to mix well.

Add tomato sauce, stirring to thicken. Add ketchup, peas, tomatoes, carrots, water and salt. Pour all into 1½-quart (1.5L) casserole. Bake uncovered in 350°F (180°C) oven for 30 minutes. Serves 3-4.

Paré Pointer

If swimming is so good for the figure, how do you account for ducks?

CHINESE CHOW

Ever wonder how to use those whole pea pods in cooking? Try this for a sure hit.

Ground beef	1½ lbs.	750 g
Chinese pea pods, frozen or fresh	7 oz. pkg.	198 g pkg.
Sliced celery	2 cups	500 mL
Chopped onion	1 cup	250 mL
Condensed tomato soup	10 oz.	284 mL
Milk	½ cup	125 mL
Salt	1 tsp.	5 mL
Pepper	¼ tsp.	1 mL
Chow mein noodles	2 cups	500 mL

Scramble fry ground beef in frying pan until well browned. Drain off fat. Spread meat in 2-quart (2L) casserole. Set aside.

Thaw pea pods. Spread over top of meat.

Slice celery on an angle. Spread over pea pods.

In medium bowl combine onion, soup, milk, salt and pepper. Mix together well. Pour over celery.

Sprinkle dry noodles over all. Cover. Bake in 350ºF (180ºC) oven for 40 minutes. Serves 6.

Pictured on page 81.

CHOP SUEY — SPANISH?

With spaghetti instead of rice, this is sure to be a preference for many.

Cooking oil	2 tbsp.	30 mL
Ground beef	1 lb.	500 g
Chopped onion	1 cup	250 mL
Chopped celery	1 cup	250 mL
Chopped green pepper	¼ cup	50 mL
Condensed tomato soup	10 oz.	284 mL
Condensed vegetable soup	10 oz.	284 mL
Sugar	1 tsp.	5 mL
Vinegar	1 tbsp.	15 mL
Ready-cut spaghetti, raw	1 cup	250 mL
Bread crumbs	½ cup	125 mL
Butter or margarine	2 tbsp.	30 mL

Heat oil in frying pan. Add beef, onion, celery and green pepper. Sauté slowly until meat is brown and vegetables are limp. Remove from heat and drain off fat.

Add tomato and vegetable soup, sugar and vinegar. Stir to mix.

Cook spaghetti according to package directions. Drain. Stir into meat mixture. Scrape into 1½-quart (1.5L) casserole.

Stir crumbs and butter together in small saucepan over medium heat until butter melts. Sprinkle over casserole. Bake uncovered in 350ºF (180ºC) oven for 30 minutes until bubbly hot. Serves 6.

CHINESE HEKKA

This is an extra good Chinese casserole. A very full flavor, it is traditionally served with lots of rice.

Ground beef	1¼ lbs.	550 g
Chopped onion	1¼ cups	300 mL
Cooking oil	2 tbsp.	30 mL
Shredded cabbage	2 cups	500 mL
Shredded carrots	2 cups	500 mL
Sliced celery	2 cups	500 mL
Soy sauce	½ cup	125 mL
Water	½ cup	125 mL

Put beef, onion, and oil into frying pan. Brown, stirring to break up meat. Drain off fat and discard. Remove from heat.

Shred cabbage using large-sized grater. Shred carrots using small-sized grater. Slice celery in thin angle slices. Add cabbage, carrots, celery, soy sauce and water to meat and onions. Scrape into 1½-quart (1.5L) casserole. Cover. Bake in 350°F (180°C) oven for 45 minutes. Serves 6.

PORCUPINES

Both tasty and showy. Because it isn't too thick it thaws quickly. Makes it freezer-right!

Ground beef	1 lb.	500 g
Chopped onion	¼ cup	50 mL
Salt	1 tsp.	5 mL
Pepper	¼ tsp.	1 mL
Long-grain rice	¼ cup	50 mL
Condensed tomato soup	10 oz.	284 mL
Soup can of water	10 oz.	284 mL

(continued on next page)

In medium-sized bowl, mix meat, onion, salt, pepper and rice together well. Shape into 25 meatballs. Arrange evenly in square baking dish.

Combine soup and water. Pour over meatballs. Cover. Bake in 350°F (180°C) oven for 1 hour or until rice is cooked. Serves 4.

VIENNESE PUFF

Serve this as a second meat. It goes with any meat. Or use as a main dish. Very unusual.

Bread crumbs	1 cup	250 mL
Sausage meat	1 lb.	500 g
Butter or margarine	3 tbsp.	50 mL
Curry powder	¼ tsp.	1 mL
Salt	½ tsp.	2 mL
Pepper	½ tsp.	2 mL
Small onion, chopped	1	1
Grated Cheddar cheese	½ cup	125 mL
Flour	½ cup	125 mL
Milk	1 cup	250 mL
Egg, fork beaten	1	1

Sprinkle crumbs evenly over bottom of baking dish about 8 x 8-inches (20 x 20 cm). Pat sausage meat on waxed paper to size of dish. Invert over crumbs and remove paper. Cover. Bake in 350°F (180°C) oven for 30 minutes. Drain off as much fat as you can manage without disturbing meat.

While meat is cooking, melt butter in medium-sized saucepan. Add curry, salt, pepper, onion and cheese. Stir until cheese is melted. Stir in flour. Add milk and beaten egg. Stir vigorously until thickened. It will be thick. Remove from heat.

When ready, remove sausage meat from oven. Drain. Spread mixture evenly over the meat. Leave uncovered. Return to oven and bake at 400°F (205°C) for 30 minutes until golden brown. Serves 3-4. As a second meat, cut into 9 pieces. Recipe can be doubled and baked in 9 x 13-inch (22 x 33 cm) pan for more servings yet.

BURGER CORN CASSEROLE

Every family likes this. The cream corn rather than niblet blends right in.

Cooking oil	2 tbsp.	30 mL
Ground beef	1½ lbs.	750 g
Large onion, chopped	1	1
Salt	1½ tsp.	7 mL
Pepper	½ tsp.	2 mL
Can cream corn	14 oz.	398 mL
Condensed tomato soup	10 oz.	284 mL
Can tomato sauce	7½ oz.	213 mL
Cooked noodles	3 cups	750 mL
Grated Cheddar cheese	1 cup	250 mL

Heat oil in frying pan. Add next 4 ingredients. Fry slowly until all pink color has disappeared from meat.

Add corn, soup and tomato sauce. Stir.

Cook noodles as directed on package. Drain. Measure. Stir into meat mixture. Pour into 3-quart (3½L) casserole.

Sprinkle with cheese. Bake in 350ºF (180ºC) oven for 1 hour. Cover at half time if cheese dries too much. Serves 6.

HAMBURGER PACIFIC

Here is a hamburger dish different from many. Delicious.

Cooking oil	2 tbsp.	30 mL
Ground beef	2 lbs.	1 kg
Medium onion, chopped	1	1
Garlic powder or minced garlic clove	¼ tsp.	1 mL
Salt	2 tsp.	10 mL
Pepper	½ tsp.	2 mL

(continued on next page)

Sliced mushrooms, drained	10 oz.	284 mL
Condensed tomato soup	10 oz.	284 mL
Cream corn	14 oz.	398 mL
Fresh chop suey vegetables	2 cups	500 mL
Cooked noodles	3 cups	750 mL

Paprika

Heat oil in frying pan. Add next 5 ingredients. Sauté until no trace of pink remains in meat. Turn off heat. Drain and discard fat.

Add mushrooms, soup and corn to meat. Stir. Transfer to 2-quart (2.5L) casserole.

Spread chop suey vegetables over meat mixture.

Prepare noodles as directed on package. Drain. Measure. Arrange over vegetables. Sprinkle with paprika for color. Cover. Bake in 350°F (180°C) oven for 40 minutes until hot. Serves 8.

WIENERS AND BEANS

Good for the rush hours.

Chopped onion	¼ cup	50 mL
Butter or margarine	1 tbsp.	15 mL
Beans in tomato sauce or pork and beans	2 — 14 oz.	2 — 398 mL
Wieners, sliced crosswise	8	8
Prepared mustard	1 tsp.	5 mL
Celery Seed	1 tsp.	5 mL

Sauté onion in butter in frying pan until onion is clear and limp.

Add beans, wieners, mustard and celery salt. Pour into 2-quart (2L) casserole. Bake uncovered in 350°F (180°C) oven for 40 minutes. Stir at half time. Serves 6.

CHEESE AND PASTA IN A POT

A good dish for a party. Have it ready in the refrigerator then pop it in the oven and join the party. When you have made it once the length of the recipe seems cut in half the second time.

Large shell macaroni	8 oz.	225 g
Ground beef	2 lbs.	1 kg
Medium onions, chopped	2	2
Garlic powder	¼ tsp.	1 mL
Canned stewed tomatoes	14 oz.	398 mL
Canned spaghetti sauce	14 oz.	398 mL
Mushroom pieces and juice	10 oz.	284 mL
Sour cream	2 cups	500 mL
Medium Cheddar cheese	½ lb.	250 g
Mozzarella cheese	½ lb.	250 g

Cook macaroni according to package directions. Rinse with cold water. Drain. Set aside.

Brown beef in frying pan. Drain and put in large saucepan such as a Dutch oven. Add onions, garlic, tomatoes, spaghetti sauce, mushrooms and juice. Bring to boil and allow to simmer 20 minutes until onions are tender. Stir occasionally while boiling. Remove from heat. Use 4-quart (5L) casserole or roaster.

Construction:
1. Pour one half macaroni in bottom of casserole
2. Pour over one half meat sauce
3. Spread with one half sour cream
4. Slice Cheddar cheese thinly and layer half on top
5. Cover with second half of macaroni
6. Spoon over second half of meat sauce
7. Spread with second half of sour cream
8. Cover with remaining thin slices of Cheddar cheese
9. Top with thin slices of mozzarella cheese

Cover. Bake in 350° F (180° C) oven for 45 minutes. Remove cover. Continue baking until cheese is melted. Allow more baking time if chilled and held. Serves 12.

CORNED BEEF AND CABBAGE

This well-known dish is easily made from a can. Creamy good.

Small cabbage	1	1
Butter or margarine	2 tbsp.	30 mL
Chopped onion	¼ cup	50 mL
Canned corned beef	12 oz.	340 g
Butter or margarine	3 tbsp.	50 mL
All-purpose flour	3 tbsp.	50 mL
Milk	1½ cups	400 mL
Salt	½ tsp.	5 mL
Pepper	⅛ tsp.	½ mL
Butter or margarine for topping	2 tbsp.	30 mL
Bread crumbs	1 cup	250 mL

Cut cabbage in half. Cut each half into 3 pieces. Remove core. Boil in salted water for 20 minutes. Drain. Put in bottom of 1½-quart (1.5L) casserole.

Melt butter in frying pan. Add onion and corned beef. Sauté, breaking up beef, until onions are clear. Pour over cabbage.

In medium-sized saucepan, melt butter. Stir in flour. Add milk, salt and pepper. Bring to a boil, stirring. Pour over meat.

In small saucepan melt butter. Stir in crumbs to blend. Sprinkle over top. Bake uncovered in 350°F (180°C) oven for 30 minutes. Serves 6.

BEEF STROGANOFF

This is the best way to use leftover roast beef. Or chicken. Or turkey. Or pork. Just delicious!

Sliced mushrooms and juice	10 oz.	284 mL
Condensed cream of mushroom soup	10 oz.	284 mL
Sour cream	2 cups	500 mL
Water	3 cups	750 mL
Dry onion flakes (or small onion, chopped)	¼ cup	50 mL
Dry beef in a mug instant soup mix	¼ cup	50 mL
Parsley flakes	2 tsp.	10 mL
Paprika	¼ tsp.	2 mL
Salt	1 tsp.	5 mL
Pepper	¼ tsp.	1 mL
Cornstarch	2 tbsp.	30 mL
Water	½ cup	50 mL
Cooked beef, cut in bite-sized pieces (approximately)	4 cups	900 mL

In large pot combine all first 10 ingredients. Bring to boil over medium heat and simmer.

Mix cornstarch with water. Stir into simmering sauce, stirring until thickened.

Add cut beef. Stir to combine. Pour into large casserole or small roaster. Bake uncovered in 350°F (180°C) oven for 45 minutes or more. Serves 6-8.

1. BBQ Pork Chops page 104
2. Chow Chow page 130
3. Carman's Caper page 66

Eaten with gusto, this is a chunky stew prepared on top of the stove.

Cooking oil	3 tbsp.	45 mL
Stewing beef, cut up	2 lbs.	1 kg
Medium onions, quartered	6	6
Oregano leaves	1 tsp.	5 mL
Rosemary leaves	1 tsp.	5 mL
Chili powder	1 tsp.	5 mL
Seasoned salt	1½ tsp.	7 mL
Salt	1 tsp.	5 mL
All-purpose flour	1 tbsp.	15 mL
Tomato paste	5½ oz.	156 mL
Water	1 cup	250 mL
Canned tomatoes	28 oz.	796 mL
Parsley leaves, fresh	½ cup	125 mL
Large carrots, thickly sliced	3	3
Celery sticks, thickly sliced	4	4
Macaroni, raw	2¼ cups	500 mL

Heat oil in frying pan. Brown beef. Transfer to large pot.

Peel and cut onions in quarters. Brown in frying pan. Transfer to pot.

Measure oregano, rosemary, chili, seasoned salt, salt and flour into medium-sized bowl. Stir well. Add next 4 ingredients. Mix together and add to meat. Bring to boil. Simmer covered for 1 hour, 20 minutes.

Add carrots and celery to meat. Simmer covered 45 minutes until vegetables and meat are tender.

Cook macaroni as directed on package. Drain. Add to meat mixture. Serves 8.

Pictured on page 117.

CARMAN'S CAPER

Just a real good anytime casserole. Quick and easy to assemble.

Ground beef	1½ lbs.	750 g
Chopped onion	½ cup	125 mL
Salt	1½ tsp.	7 mL
Pepper	¼ tsp.	1 mL
Spaghetti	½ lb.	250 g
Canned tomatoes	19 oz.	540 mL
Condensed cream of mushroom soup	10 oz.	284 mL
Grated Cheddar cheese	1 cup	250 mL

Brown beef and onion in frying pan. Sprinkle with salt and pepper. Stir. Transfer to bottom of 2-quart (2L) casserole.

Break up spaghetti for easier serving. Cook according to package directions. Drain. Layer over meat.

Break up large tomato chunks. Pour over top. Spoon soup over tomatoes. Cover with cheese. Bake uncovered in 350°F (180°F) oven for 30 minutes until hot and cheese is melted. Cover halfway through cooking if cheese starts getting dry. Serves 6.

Pictured on page 63.

SHORT RIBS

Who would have thought you could make company fare from plain short ribs?

Short ribs	3-4 lbs.	1.4-1.8 kg
Tomato sauce	7½ oz.	213 mL

(continued on next page)

Salt	1½ tsp.	7 mL
Pepper	½ tsp.	2 mL
Dried onion flakes	1 tbsp.	15 mL
Molasses	2 tbsp.	30 mL
Vinegar	2 tbsp.	30 mL

Place ribs into large casserole or medium roaster.

SAUCE
Combine all sauce ingredients in small bowl. Mix together well. Pour over ribs. Cover. Bake in 300°F (160°C) oven for 4-5 hours until tender. Remove meat to serving bowl. Tip pan slightly and skim off fat before dishing sauce over top. Serves 4.

Pictured on page 9.

SHEPHERDS' PIE

An old favorite made to use leftovers in tasty fashion.

Cooked roast beef, ground	3 cups	700 mL
Small onion, ground	1	1
Beef gravy	½-1 cup	125-250 mL
Salt	1 tsp.	5 mL
Pepper	¼ tsp.	1 mL
Mashed potatoes	3 cups	700 mL

Put beef and onion through food chopper. If you don't have one, chop with knife into very small pieces.

Add gravy. Mix well. Should be pasty enough to hold together. Pack in 9 x 9-inch (23 x 23 cm) pan. Adjust seasoning.

Spread potatoes over top of meat. Bake uncovered in 350°F (180°C) oven for 30 minutes until hot and potatoes are brown. Serves 4.

CHILI CON CARNE

This is a meaty stove top casserole, very easy to make. The flavor of chili is quite mild and can be quickly increased for a stronger flavor.

Cooking oil	2 tbsp.	30 mL
Large onions, chopped	2	2
Ground beef	2 lbs.	1 kg
Canned red kidney beans	2 − 14 oz.	2 − 398 mL
Condensed tomato soup	2 − 10 oz.	2 − 284 mL
Chili powder	1 tsp.	5 mL
Granulated Sugar	2 tbsp.	30 mL
Salt	2 tsp.	10 mL
Pepper	¼ tsp.	1 mL
Accent	1 tsp.	5 mL

Heat oil in pan. Sauté onions. Add beef and continue to cook until no trace of pink remains. Transfer to large pot.

Add beans and soup to large pot. Mix together. Sprinkle with chili, sugar, salt, pepper and accent. Stir. Simmer for about 15 minutes checking seasoning. Add water if needed. Can be transferred to casserole to put in oven when needed. Serves 8.

MEAT-ZA-PIE

Packed full of flavor. Good party dish.

Ground beef	1 lb.	500 g
Milk	⅔ cup	150 mL
Bread crumbs	½ cup	125 mL
Garlic salt	½ tsp.	2 mL
Tomato paste or ketchup	⅓ cup	75 mL
Oregano	¼ tsp.	1 mL

(continued on next page)

68

Sliced mushrooms, drained	10 oz.	284 mL
Medium Cheddar cheese, grated	1 cup	250 mL
Grated Parmesan cheese	2 tbsp.	30 mL

In medium-sized bowl combine beef, milk, crumbs and garlic. Mix well. Pat in 9 x 9-inch (23 x 23 cm) pan.

Stir tomato paste and oregano together. Spread over meat.

Drain mushrooms and sprinkle over top.

Sprinkle Cheddar cheese over mushrooms.

Sprinkle Parmesan cheese over top. Bake uncovered in 375°F (190°C) oven for 35-45 minutes. Serves 4 as a main dish and 8 as a second.

WIENER WINNER

For a complete meal in one, try this supper dish.

Potatoes, thinly sliced	2-3	2-3
Onion, thinly sliced	1	1
Carrots, thinly sliced	2-3	2-3
Long-grain rice, raw	¼ cup	50 mL
Peas, frozen or fresh	1 cup	250 mL
Wieners	1 lb.	500 g
Condensed tomato soup	10 oz.	284 mL
Can of water	10 oz.	284 mL

Arrange layers in order given in 2-quart (2L) casserole. Put wieners on top.

Combine soup with water. Pour over top of wieners. Cover. Bake 2 hours in 350°F (180°C) oven until vegetables are tender. Serves 4.

SHEPHERD'S PIE SIMPLISTIC

No leftover meat! Try this hamburger version of an old favorite.

Ground beef	1 lb.	500 g
Cooking oil	2 tbsp.	30 mL
Chopped celery	½ cup	125 mL
Chopped onion	½ cup	125 mL
All-purpose flour	2 tbsp.	30 mL
Salt	1 tsp.	5 mL
Pepper	¼ tsp.	1 mL
Boiling water	1 cup	250 mL
Beef bouillon cube	1	1
Mashed potatotes	3 cups	700 mL

Combine beef, oil, celery and onion in frying pan. Scramble fry until brown.

Stir in flour, salt and pepper.

Pour boiling water over bouillon cube. Dissolve. Pour into meat mixture. Stir until boiling and thickened. Spread in 1½-quart (1.5L) casserole.

Cover with potatoes. Bake uncovered in 350ºF (180ºC) oven for 30 minutes until heated through and potatoes are browned. Serves 4.

Paré Pointer

When a whole orchestra goes on welfare it is called band-aid.

Especially good for a ladies' luncheon. Also ideal for a gourmet second meat when putting on a "spread".

Thin slices of square cooked ham loaf	14	14
Prepared mustard		
Canned asparagus spears, drained	2 — 10 oz.	2 — 284 mL
Butter or margarine	3 tbsp.	45 mL
All-purpose flour	2 tbsp.	30 mL
Milk	1½ cups	350 mL
Salt	¾ tsp.	3 mL
Pepper	¼ tsp.	1 mL
Grated medium Cheddar cheese	1 cup	250 mL
Green onions, very thinly sliced in rings	¼ cup	50 mL

Spread each slice of ham with mustard. Lay 3 asparagus spears on each slice, alternating tips for appearance and ease of rolling. Roll up and arrange in casserole seam side down.

Melt butter in medium-sized saucepan. Stir in flour. Add milk. Stir and cook until boiling. Add salt and pepper. Stir in cheese until melted. Add green onions. Stir and pour over meat rolls. Cover. Bake in 350°F (180°C) oven for 20 minutes or until hot and bubbly. Serves 14 as a second meat dish or 5-6 as a main dish. Fresh asparagus may be used. It takes longer to cook but is such a pretty green.

Pictured on page 45.

Truth may be stranger than fiction but it is also more decent.

MEATBALLS IN MUSHROOM SOUP

Creamy meatballs are welcome anytime.

Condensed cream of mushroom soup	10 oz.	284 mL
Water	½ cup	125 mL
Ground beef	1 lb.	500 g
Bread crumbs	⅓ cup	75 mL
Soup and water mixture	⅓ cup	75 mL
Minced onion	2 tbsp.	30 mL
Parsley flakes	1 tbsp.	15 mL
Egg	1	1

In small bowl stir together soup and water. Set aside.

In large bowl combine beef, crumbs, ⅓ cup (75 mL) of soup mixture, onion, parsley and egg. Mix together well. Shape into balls or patties. Brown all sides and arrange in casserole. Cover with remaining soup mixture. Bake covered in 350°F (180°C) oven for 35-45 minutes until meat is finished cooking. Serves 4.

ONE-DISH MEAL

Here is a complete meal with sausages.

Potatoes, sliced	2-3	2-3
Onion, sliced	1	1
Carrots, sliced	2-3	2-3
Potatoes, sliced	2-3	2-3
Onion, sliced	1	1
Carrots, sliced	2-3	2-3
Frozen peas	1 cup	250 mL
Small pork sausage	1 lb.	500 g

(continued on next page)

Condensed tomato soup	10 oz.	284 mL
Can of water	10 oz.	284 mL

Layer thinly sliced peeled potatoes over bottom of deep 2-quart (2L) casserole. Add layers in order given, slicing thinly. Spread peas over. Arrange sausage on top. If you first prick and boil sausage for 10 minutes, much of the fat is removed.

Mix soup and water together. Pour over all. Cover. Bake in 350°F (180°C) oven for 1 hour. Remove cover. Turn sausages and bake uncovered 1 hour until the vegetables are tender. Serves 4.

WIENER CHEESE DISH

A different and tasty method to use wieners either for a luncheon or a heavier meal.

Wieners	12	12
Cheese wedges or cut slices	12	12
Bacon slices	12	12
Dry onion flakes	1 tbsp.	15 mL
Canned stewed tomatoes containing onions, celery, etc.	14 oz.	398 mL

Split wieners lengthways not cutting quite through. Insert cheese in each. Beginning at one end, wrap slice of bacon around wiener in diagonal fashion, securing with toothpick at both ends. Arrange in 9 x 13-inch (23 x 33 cm) cake pan. Broil until brown.

Stir onion flakes into tomatoes. Pour over meat. Bake uncovered in 350°F (180°C) oven for 20 minutes until hot. Serves 4.

SIMPLE PATTY

About the most economical hamburger casserole going. It has a milk gravy. Tasty and nutritious.

Ground beef	2 lbs.	1 kg
Bread crumbs	1 cup	250 mL
Water	1 cup	250 mL
Salt	2 tsp.	10 mL
Pepper	½ tsp.	2 mL
Instant onion flakes (optional)	2 tbsp.	30 mL
All-purpose flour	6 tbsp.	100 mL
Butter or margarine	4-6 tbsp.	60-100 mL
Salt	1 tsp.	5 mL
Milk	4 cups	900 mL
Water	1 cup	250 mL

Combine first 5 or 6 ingredients in large bowl. Mix together well. Shape into patties. Brown well on both sides removing to casserole as finished. The idea is to brown them, not necessarily cook them.

Stir flour into fat in pan. Add as much butter as needed to combine with flour. Stir in salt. Pour in milk, stirring until boiling and thickened. Stir in water. Scrape all brown bits off pan into gravy. Pour over patties. Cover. Bake in 350°F (180°C) oven for 1 hour. Serves 6-8.

HAMBURGER PATTY CASSEROLE

This can be made ahead. Reheats beautifully with a tasty gravy.

Ground beef	2½ lbs.	1.1 kg
Envelope dry onion soup mix	1½ oz.	42.5 g
Bread crumbs	1 cup	250 mL

(continued on next page)

Water	1 cup	250 mL
Salt	½ tsp.	2 mL
Condensed tomato soup	2 — 10 oz.	2 — 284 mL
Cans of water	2 — 10 oz.	2 — 284 mL
Mushroom pieces and juice	10 oz.	284 mL

Put first 5 ingredients into large bowl. Using your hand, mix together well. Shape into patties. Brown both sides in frying pan. Remove to baking dish.

Stir soup and water together in medium bowl. Stir in mushrooms and juice. Pour over meat. Bake covered in 350°F (180°C) oven for 1 hour. Serves 8.

SAUCY MEATBALLS

Quick and easy with a difference.

Ground beef	1¼ lbs.	560 g
Bread crumbs	½ cup	125 mL
Water	½ cup	125 mL
Salt	1 tsp.	5 mL
Pepper	¼ tsp.	1 mL
Condensed tomato soup	10 oz.	284 mL
Horseradish	½ tsp.	2 mL
Worcestershire sauce	1 tsp.	5 mL

In large bowl, mix first 5 ingredients. Shape into balls. Brown in frying pan. Remove to 1½-quart (1.5L) casserole.

In same bowl combine soup, horseradish and Worcestershire sauce. Pour over meatballs. Cover. Bake in 350°F (180°C) oven for 35 minutes. Serves 4.

POLPETTONI PAT

This is good but fussy to make. Allow some extra time to prepare.

Ground beef	2 lbs.	1 kg
Minced onion	⅓ cup	75 mL
Salt	1 tsp.	5 mL
Oregano	¼ tsp.	1 mL
Egg, slightly beaten	1	1
Spaghetti sauce with mushrooms	¼ cup	50 mL
Cooked rice	1½ cups	400 mL
Minced green pepper	⅓ cup	75 mL
Spaghetti sauce	¼ cup	50 mL
Spaghetti sauce	½ cup	125 mL
Spaghetti sauce	1 cup	225 mL

In large bowl, mix first 6 ingredients together. Press out mixture on waxed paper into rectangle 7 x 12-inches (23 x 30 cm). Cut crosswise into 6, 7-inch strips. Set aside.

Combine rice, green pepper and ¼ cup (50 mL) spaghetti sauce. Divide into 6 portions putting on one-half of each meat strip. Carefully fold meat over, shaping each into loaf. Put in baking pan.

Spoon ½ cup (125 mL) sauce over meat loaves. Bake uncovered in 350°F (180°C) oven for 25 minutes. Spoon remaining sauce over loaves. Bake about 10 minutes more. Rice will spill out if you bake too long. Serves 6.

GIBSON STEW

Once you assemble everything in one pan in the oven, the whole afternoon is free.

Stewing meat, cut up	2 lbs.	1 kg
Onion, sliced	1	1
Celery sticks in 1 inch (2 cm) slices	6	6
Carrots in 1 inch (2 cm) slices	6	6
Potatoes, cut in chunks	4	4
Salt	2 tsp.	10 mL
Pepper	¼ tsp.	1 mL
Sugar	1 tbsp.	15 mL
Monosodium glutamate	1 tsp.	5 mL
Minute tapioca	3 tbsp.	45 mL
Tomato juice	1½ cups	375 mL

Combine first 5 ingredients in casserole or roaster.

Mix salt, pepper, sugar, monosodium glutamate and tapioca in bowl. Stir. Add tomato juice. Stir. Pour over meat and vegetables. Cover. Bake in 300°F (150°C) oven for 4 hours until tender. Serves 6-8.

OVEN STEW

Similar to, but with a different flavor combination than Gibson Stew. Can easily be doubled.

Stewing beef, cut up	1 lb.	500 g
Large onion, cut up	1	1
Potatoes, cut up	1-2	1-2
Carrots, cut up	1-2	1-2
Tomato sauce	7½ oz.	213 mL
Beef broth or bouillon	½ cup	125 mL
Salt	¾ tsp.	6 mL
Pepper	⅛ tsp.	0.5 mL

Combine all together in casserole or roaster. Cover. Bake in 300°F (150°C) oven for 3½-4 hours until tender. Serves 4.

STEAK AND MUSHROOM CASSEROLE

Have your steak cooking with no last minute attention.

All-purpose flour	⅓ cup	75 mL
Salt	2 tsp.	10 mL
Pepper	¼ tsp.	1 mL
Dry mustard	1 tbsp.	15 mL
Sirloin steak, cubed	2 lbs.	1 kg
Cooking oil	4 tbsp.	60 mL
Sliced mushrooms	2½ cups	550 mL
Medium onion, cut up	1	1
White wine or apple cider	2 tbsp.	30 mL
Brown sugar	3 tbsp.	45 mL
Worcestershire sauce	1½ tbsp.	25 mL
Canned tomatoes	19 oz.	540 mL

Mix first 4 ingredients together.

Either cube or strip-cut meat. Coat damp meat with flour mixture. Heat oil in frying pan. Brown beef cubes well. Transfer to 2-quart (2L) casserole.

Add rest of ingredients. Cover. Bake in 350°F (180°C) oven for 1½-2 hours until tender. Serves 6

SWISS STEAK

An economical way to cook round steak. A good make-ahead.

Round steak	2 lbs.	1 kg
Cooking oil	2 tbsp.	30 mL
Salt		
Pepper		

(continued on next page)

Medium onions	1-2	1-2
Butter or margarine	¼ cup	50 mL
All-purpose flour	¼ cup	50 mL
Salt	1 tsp.	5 mL
Pepper	¼ tsp.	1 mL
Water	4 cups	900 mL

Cut meat in serving-size pieces. Heat oil in frying pan. Brown meat on both sides over medium-high heat. Sprinkle with salt and pepper. Put meat in large casserole or small roaster.

Peel onions. Cut into chunks. Distribute over and around meat.

Melt butter in frying pan. Stir in flour, salt and pepper. Add all at once, stirring to thicken and loosen all bits stuck to the pan. At this point you may want to add gravy coloring if needed for color. Have gravy quite thin. It will thicken as it cooks and boils down. Taste and add more seasoning if needed. Pour over meat and onions. Bake covered at 350°F (180°C) oven for 1½-2 hours or until fork tender. Serves 4-6.

QUICK CASSEROLE

Just brown it, sauce it and bake it.

Cooking oil	2 tbsp.	30 mL
Round steak	2 lbs.	1 kg
Condensed cream of mushroom soup	10 oz.	284 mL
Water	¼ cup	50 mL

Cut meat into serving-size pieces or leave whole. Brown in heated oil in frying pan. Transfer to casserole or small roaster.

In small bowl, combine soup with water. Pour over top of meat. Cover. Bake in 350°F (180°C) oven for 1-1½ hours or until tender. Serves 5-6.

SWISS STEAK DELUXE

Good anytime but especially when fresh vegetables are in season.

Round steak	2 lbs.	1 kg
Cooking oil	2 tbsp.	30 mL
Salt	1 tsp.	5 mL
Pepper	½ tsp.	2 mL
Condensed tomato soup	10 oz.	284 mL
Soup can of water	10 oz.	284 mL
Small potatoes	8-12	8-12
Small onions	8-12	8-12
Small carrots	8-12	8-12

Cut steak into serving-size pieces. Brown in heated oil. Sprinkle with salt and pepper. Transfer to large casserole or small roaster.

Stir soup and water together. Pour over meat.

Clean vegetables and add to sauce. Cover. Bake in 350°F (180°C) oven for 1 ½ hours until meat and potatoes are tender. Serves 5-6.

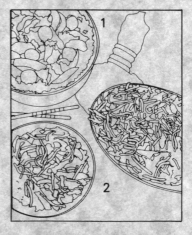

1. Turkey Chow Mein page 15
2. Chinese Chow page 54

A delicious pork dish dressed up with fruit.

Lean pork, cubed	2 lbs.	1 kg
All-purpose flour	2-4 tbsp.	30-60 mL
Cooking oil	3 tbsp.	45 mL
Orange juice	1 cup	225 mL
Lemon juice	2 tbsp.	30 mL
Worcestershire sauce	1 tbsp.	15 mL
Brown sugar, packed	3 tbsp.	50 mL
Salt	1 tsp.	5 mL
Pepper	¼ tsp.	1 mL
Cornstarch	1 tbsp.	15 mL
Water	¼ cup	50 mL
Raisins	⅓ cup	75 mL
Orange sections, drained	10 oz.	284 mL

Coat meat with flour. Heat oil in frying pan. Brown meat on all sides. Transfer to 2-quart (2L) casserole.

Discard fat in frying pan. Pour orange and lemon juice into pan. Add Worcestershire sauce, sugar, salt and pepper.

Stir cornstarch into water. Pour into juice stirring as you bring to boil. Pour over meat.

Add raisins and orange sections. Stir lightly. Cover. Bake in 350ºF (180ºC) oven for 1½-2 hours until cooked through and very tender. Serves 6.

BAKED SWISS

No browning for this one. Add baked potatoes and you have a meal.

Round steak, cut	2 lbs.	1 kg
Envelope dry onion soup	1	1
Sliced mushrooms, drained	10 oz.	284 mL
Chopped green peppers	¼ cup	50 mL
Canned tomatoes	14 oz.	398 mL
Bottled steak sauce	1 tbsp.	15 mL
Minute tapioca	1 tbsp.	15 mL
Parsley flakes	1 tsp.	5 mL

Cut meat in serving-size pieces. Arrange in 2-quart (2L) casserole. Sprinkle dry soup over. Spread mushrooms over top. Sprinkle green peppers over. In small bowl stir tomatoes, sauce, tapioca and parsley. Pour over meat. Cover. Bake in 350°F (180°C) oven for 2 hours until tender. Serves 6-8.

GOLDEN SAUSAGES

A snappy little dish from New Zealand.

Small pork sausages	1 lb.	500 g
Water		
Tomato sauce	6 tbsp.	100 mL
All-purpose flour	6 tbsp.	100 mL
Vinegar	6 tbsp.	100 mL
Granulated sugar	3 tbsp.	50 mL
Worcestershire sauce	2 tbsp.	30 mL
Boiling water	2 cups	500 mL
Grated carrots	1 cup	250 mL
Grated onion	⅓ cup	75 mL
Parsley flakes	1 tsp.	5 mL
Potatoes, peeled	2-3	2-3

(continued on next page)

Prick sausages and put in medium-sized saucepan. Add water, enough to cover sausages. Boil for 10 minutes to remove fat. Drain. Put in bowl. Set aside.

In same saucepan, stir tomato sauce, flour and vinegar together briskly until flour is blended in. Add sugar, Worcestershire sauce and boiling water. Bring to boil, stirring constantly until thickened.

Add carrots, onions and parsley. Pour in 1½-quart (1.5L) casserole. Cover with sausages. Cover. Bake in 350°F (180°C) oven for 45 minutes. Remove from oven.

Cover with sliced potatoes. Continue to bake, covered, for 1 hour or until potatoes are tender. Serves 4.

SWEET AND SOUR SAUSAGES

This turns the lowly sausage into something extra special.

Small pork sausages	2 lbs.	1 kg
Canned sliced peaches	14 oz.	398 mL
Granulated sugar	¾ cup	175 mL
Curry powder	1 tsp.	5 mL
Onion flakes	1 tbsp.	15 mL
Chili sauce	1 cup	250 mL
Ketchup	½ cup	125 mL

Brown sausages, not necessarily cook, in frying pan or under broiler. Cut in bite-sized pieces or use cocktail sausages. Place in 1½-quart (1.5L) casserole.

Add remaining ingredients. Stir together. Bake uncovered in 350°F (180°C) oven for 30 minutes. Stir. Continue to bake for 15-20 minutes until sausages are well done. Serves 8.

Pictured on cover.

TOP OF THE STOVE STEW

A good basic stew. If you want to add extras, the choice is yours. Colorful.

Stewing meat, cut up	2 lbs.	1 kg
Cooking oil	2 tbsp.	30 mL
Boiling water	3-4 cups	700 mL
Salt	2 tsp.	10 mL
Pepper	¼ tsp.	1 mL
Medium onions, cut up	2	2
Cut up potatoes	3 cups	750 mL
Cut up carrots	2 cups	500 mL
Frozen peas	1 cup	250 mL

Put meat and oil in large heavy pot. Brown meat. Pour water over top almost covering meat. Add salt and pepper. Cover. Bring to boil. Allow to simmer for 1½ hours until tender.

Cut onions in fairly large pieces. Add to meat. Peel and cut potatoes. Add to pot. Peel carrots. Cut in pieces not quite as large as potatoes. Add. Cover. Bring to boil again. Allow to simmer for 30 minutes until vegetables are tender.

Stir in peas. Bring to boil once more. If stew appears too dry, add more water. Remove from heat. Serves 6-8.

Paré Pointer

Don't ever challenge anyone to a battle of wits. They may be unarmed.

Rice is added raw to save a step. The crackers make an unusual crust.

Round crackers (such as Ritz)

Sausage meat	1 lb.	500 g
Chopped onion	¾ cup	175 mL
Long-grain rice	⅓ cup	175 mL
Water	1 cup	250 mL
Shredded Cheddar cheese	1 cup	250 mL
Round crackers		
Milk	1½ cups	375 mL
Eggs, fork beaten	3	3

Cover bottom in 1½-quart (1.5L) casserole with crackers.

Brown meat and onion in frying pan. Drain and discard fat. Add rice and water to meat mixture. Stir and pour carefully over crackers.

Sprinkle with cheese. Cover with layer of crackers.

Mix milk and eggs together well. Pour slowly over top. Bake uncovered in 350°F (180°C) oven for about 1 hour. Serves 4.

Paré Pointer

Before calling a college freshman an ignorant kid, try writing an entrance exam.

SHIPWRECK

An old favorite you no doubt grew up with.

Large onions	2	2
Medium potatoes	2	2
Ground beef	1 lb.	500 g
Long-grain rice	½ cup	125 mL
Chopped celery	1 cup	125 mL
Salt and pepper		
Condensed cream of tomato soup	10 oz.	284 mL
Can boiling water	10 oz.	284 mL

Peel onions and slice over bottom of 2-quart (2.5L) casserole. Sprinkle with salt and pepper. Slice peeled potatoes over onions. Salt and pepper potatoes. Pat ground beef over. Sprinkle with salt and pepper. Sprinkle rice on next, followed by celery. Sprinkle with salt and pepper.

Mix soup and water together. Pour over top. Bake covered in 350°F (180°C) oven for 2 hours until vegetables are tender. Serves 4.

LAZY PEROGY CASSEROLE

Different fillings are combined. If you prefer one special filling, omit the other.

Lasagne noodles	15	15
Cottage cheese	2 cups	500 mL
Egg	1	1
Onion salt	¼ tsp.	1 mL
Shredded Cheddar cheese	1 cup	250 mL
Mashed potato	2 cups	500 mL
Salt	¼ tsp.	1 mL
Onion salt	¼ tsp.	1 mL
Pepper	⅛ tsp.	0.5 mL

(continued on next page)

Butter or margarine	1 cup	250 mL
Chopped onions	1 cup	250 mL

Cook noodles as directed on package. Drain. Line bottom of 9 x 13-inch (22 x 33 cm) pan.

In medium-sized bowl, mix cottage cheese, egg and onion salt together. Spoon over noodles and spread. Cover with layer of noodles.

In same bowl, mix Cheddar cheese with potato, salt, onion salt and pepper. Spread over noodles. Cover with layer of noodles.

Melt butter in frying pan. Sauté onions slowly until clear and soft. Pour over noodles. Cover. Bake 30 minutes in 350°F (180°C) oven. Let stand 10 minutes before cutting. Serve with sour cream. Makes 8 large servings.

MARITIME MADNESS

Plain dish goes wild! You will love the seasoning.

Ground beef	1 lb.	500 g
Condensed cream of mushroom soup	10 oz.	284 mL
Chopped onions	½ cup	125 mL
Parsley flakes	1 tbsp.	15 mL
Salt	1 tsp.	5 mL
Pepper	¼ tsp.	1 mL
Sage	½ tsp.	2 mL
Ketchup	3 tbsp.	50 mL
Barbecue sauce	1 tbsp.	15 mL
Garlic powder	½ tsp.	2 mL
Rolled oats	½ cup	125 mL

Combine all ingredients in large bowl. Mix together well. Pat down in 1½-quart (1.5L) casserole. Bake covered 50 minutes 350°F (180°C). Remove cover and bake about 15 minutes to brown. Serves 4.

PINEAPPLE MEATBALLS

A sweet and sour combination with a tangy flavour, and the rice comes from the soup.

Ground beef	1½ lbs.	750 g
Bread crumbs	½ cup	125 mL
Water	½ cup	125 mL
Salt	1½ tsp.	7 mL
Pepper	¼ tsp.	1 mL
Pineapple tidbits, reserving syrup	14 oz.	398 mL
Chopped green pepper (optional)	½ cup	125 mL
Condensed chicken with rice soup	10 oz.	284 mL
Soy sauce	1 tbsp.	15 mL
Sugar	½ cup	125 mL
Pineapple juice	½ cup	125 mL
Vinegar	½ cup	125 mL
Cornstarch	3 tbsp.	45 mL

Put first 5 ingredients in bowl. Mix together well. Shape into small balls. Brown. Remove to 2-quart (2.5L) casserole.

In medium-sized saucepan, combine pineapple, green pepper, soup, soy sauce, sugar and pineapple juice. Bring to boil.

Stir cornstarch in vinegar. Stir to make smooth. Add to boiling mixture stirring and cooking until thickened. Pour over meatballs. Cover. Bake in 350°F (180°C) oven for 30 minutes. Serves 6.

Paré Pointer

Man is known by the company he keeps, woman by how late she keeps company.

A really delicious gourmet casserole from hamburger.

Butter or margarine	2 tbsp.	30 mL
Finely chopped onion	1 cup	250 mL
Ground beef	1 lb.	500 g
All-purpose flour	2 tbsp.	30 mL
Salt	1 tsp.	5 mL
Pepper	¼ tsp.	1 mL
Sliced mushrooms, drained	10 oz.	284 mL
Condensed cream of chicken soup	10 oz.	284 mL
Sour cream	½ cup	125 mL
Grated Cheddar cheese	¼ cup	65 mL

Melt butter in frying pan. Add onions and sauté slowly until limp. Add beef stirring to break up lumps. Brown. Drain off fat. Discard.

Sprinkle flour, salt and pepper over meat mixture. Stir. Add mushrooms. Cook uncovered for 10 minutes.

Add soup. Stir. Cook uncovered for 10 minutes.

Stir in sour cream and cheese. Heat through. Can be served immediately or poured into a casserole, covered and held in warm oven. Serves 4.

Pâré Pointer

When you notice some of the body shapes today, it adds credibility to the theory of evolution.

PORK CASSEROLE

Try this for a change from the usual ground beef.

Ground pork	1 lb.	500 g
Chopped onion	½ cup	125 mL
Canned tomatoes	14 oz.	398 mL
Grated Cheddar cheese	1 cup	250 mL
Cooked egg noodles	2 cups	500 mL
Butter or margarine	2 tbsp.	30 mL
Bread crumbs	1 cup	250 mL

Brown pork and onion in frying pan. Drain off fat.

Add tomatoes and cheese. Stir.

Stir in cooked noodles. Pour into 1½-quart (1.5L) casserole.

Melt butter in small saucepan. Add crumbs. Stir to coat. Distribute evenly over top. Bake uncovered in 350°F (180°C) oven for 30 minutes until hot and crumbs are browned. Serves 4.

CHINESE NOODLE CASSEROLE

A quick meal, moist and flavorful.

Cooking oil	2 tbsp.	30 mL
Sliced celery	1 cup	250 mL
Chopped onion	1 cup	250 mL
Ground beef	1 lb.	500 g
Condensed tomato soup	10 oz.	284 mL
Condensed cream of mushroom soup	10 oz.	284 mL

(continued on next page)

Soy sauce	2 tbsp.	30 mL
Chow mein noodles	¾ of 4 oz. can	¾ of 113 g
Chow mein noodles	¼ of 4 oz. can	¼ of 113 g

Heat oil in frying pan. Add celery, onion and beef. Brown.

Add tomato soup, mushroom soup, soy sauce and noodles. Stir to combine. Pour into 1½-quart (1.5L) casserole.

Sprinkle remaining dry noodles over all. Bake uncovered in 350°F (180°C) oven for 45 minutes. Serves 4-6.

SAUCY FRANKS

This sweet and sour sauce perks up the whole dish.

Wieners	12	12
Butter or margarine	3 tbsp.	45 mL
Chopped onions	1 cup	250 mL
Chopped celery	½ cup	125 mL
Vinegar	¼ cup	60 mL
Packed brown sugar	¼ cup	60 mL
Ketchup	½ cup	125 mL
Worcestershire sauce	1 tbsp.	15 mL
Dry mustard	1 tsp.	5 mL
Water	½ cup	125 mL

Arrange wieners in bottom of square baking dish.

Melt butter in frying pan. Add onions and celery. Sauté until onions are clear.

Add next 6 ingredients and mix. Pour over wieners. Bake uncovered in 350°F (180°C) oven for 30 minutes. Serves 4.

CHEESEBURGER PIE

No prebrowning of meat. Try making with and without top crust.
Use very lean meat, otherwise prebrown.

Pastry for a 9-inch (23 cm) pie
 plate, your own or a mix.
 See page 127

Ground beef	1 lb.	500 g
Chopped onion	⅓ cup	75 mL
Water or milk	½ cup	125 mL
Bread crumbs	½ cup	125 mL
Ketchup	½ cup	125 mL
Salt	1 tsp.	5 mL
Pepper	¼ tsp.	1 mL
Oregano (optional)	¼ tsp.	1 mL
Grated Cheddar cheese	1 cup	250 mL

Roll out pastry and fit into pie plate.

In medium-sized bowl put beef, onions and water. Mix well. Add
next 5 ingredients. Mix and put into pie shell. Smooth top.

Sprinkle cheese over top. Bake covered in 350°F (180°C) oven for
45 minutes. Or cover with top crust and bake uncovered. Cut into
6 wedges.

MOUSSAKA

A shortcut version of this popular Greek dish. It still takes some
extra time to prepare but is worth every minute.

Cooking oil	½ cup	125 mL
Medium eggplants	2	2

(continued on next page)

Flour
Salt and pepper

Cooking oil	2 tbsp.	30 mL
Ground beef	1½ lbs.	700 g
Chopped onion	1 cup	250 mL
Salt	1 tsp.	5 mL
Pepper	½ tsp.	2 mL
Garlic powder (or 1 clove minced)	¼ tsp.	1 mL
Nutmeg	¼ tsp.	1 mL
Water	½ cup	125 mL
Tomato paste	5½ oz.	156 mL
Grated Parmesan cheese	¼ cup	50 mL

Mozzarella slices to cover

Heat oil in frying pan. Cut eggplants in ½ inch (1 cm) slices. Peel slices and coat with flour. Brown in hot oil. On browned sides, sprinkle with salt and pepper. Cook 5 minutes or until soft and easily cut. Set aside.

Put oil in the same pan. Add beef and onions. Scramble fry until onions are soft and meat is cooked. Remove from heat.

Sprinkle salt, pepper, garlic and nutmeg over meat. Add water, tomato sauce and Parmesan. Stir together well. Layer in 9 x 13-inch (22 x 33 cm) pan:

1. ½ eggplant slices
2. ½ meat sauce
3. ½ eggplant slices
4. ½ meat sauce
5. Mozzarella cheese

Bake uncovered in 350ºF (180ºC) oven for 30 minutes until heated through. Eggplant slices can be boiled in salted water instead of fried. Makes 8 large servings.

Pictured on page 135.

HAWAIIAN SAUSAGE

This casserole contains fried pineapple. Needs rice or fluffy mashed potatoes to accompany it.

Pork sausage	1 lb.	500 g
Pineapple rings, reserve juice	14 oz.	398 mL
Pineapple juice and water	1 cup	225 mL
Cornstarch	1 tbsp.	15 mL
Curry powder	½ tsp.	2 mL

Fry sausages in frying pan. Arrange in 8-inch (20 cm) casserole.

In same pan, brown pineapple on both sides. Cut each ring into 4 pieces. Transfer pineapple to cover sausages.

Stir cornstarch and curry into pineapple juice. Pour into sausage fat in frying pan. Stir until boiling and thickened. Pour over pineapple. Bake in 350ºF (180ºC) oven for 30-40 minutes until hot. Serves 4.

SWEET AND SOUR MEATBALLS

This fits in well as a second meat. Its tangy taste goes with anything.

Ground beef	1¼ lbs.	550 g
Bread crumbs	½ cup	125 mL
Water or milk	½ cup	125 mL
Salt	1 tsp.	5 mL
Pepper	¼ tsp.	1 mL
Packed brown sugar	2 cups	500 mL
All-purpose flour	2 tbsp.	30 mL
Vinegar	½ cup	125 mL
Water	¼ cup	65 mL

(continued on next page)

| Soy sauce | 2 tbsp. | 30 mL |
| Ketchup | 1 tbsp. | 15 mL |

In medium-sized bowl, mix beef, crumbs, water, salt and pepper. Shape into approximately 24 balls. Brown in frying pan or hot oven. Transfer to casserole.

In medium-sized saucepan put brown sugar and flour. Stir well to blend thoroughly.

Add vinegar, water, soy sauce and ketchup. Stir over medium-high heat until boiling. Pour over meatballs. Cover. Heat in 350°F (180°C) oven for 20 minutes until hot and bubbly. Serves 4.

PARTY MEAT LOAVES

Little dressed up meat loaves make a real hit.

Ground beef	2 lbs.	1 kg
Bread crumbs	⅔ cup	150 mL
Milk	⅔ cup	150 mL
Finely chopped onions	⅔ cup	150 mL
Egg	1	1
Salt	2 tsp.	10 mL
Pepper	½ tsp.	2 mL
Garlic powder	¼ tsp.	1 mL
Apricot jam	1 cup	250 mL
Cider vinegar	1 tbsp.	15 mL
Canned apricots, drained	14 oz.	398 mL

In large bowl put beef, crumbs, milk, onion, egg, salt, pepper and garlic powder. Mix together well. Shape into 6 or 8 small meat loaves. Place in flat baking dish close together.

SAUCE
Put jam and cider vinegar in blender. Blend until smooth. Spoon over loaves. Bake in 350°F (180°C) oven for 45 minutes. Baste during cooking.

Garnish with apricot halves. Serves 6-8.

FRENCH TOURTIÈRE

Really freezer handy. Individual pies can be made instead.

**Pastry for 4 crusts, your own
   or a mix. See page 127**

Ground pork	1 lb.	500 g
Ground beef	2 lbs.	1 kg
Medium onion, ground or	1	1
finely chopped		
Allspice	½ tsp.	2 mL
Pinch of cloves		
Salt	2 tsp.	10 mL
Pepper	½ tsp.	2 mL
Garlic powder	½ tsp.	2 mL
Water	1½ cups	375 mL
Bread crumbs (or 2 medium	¾ cup	175 mL
potatoes cooked and mashed)		

Roll pastry. Line pie plates. Set aside.

Put next 9 ingredients into extra large saucepan. Bring to boil. Simmer 20 minutes. Stir occasionally. Add crumbs and stir. Mixture should be moist and thick. Cool.

Line two 9-inch (23 cm) pie plates with pastry. Fill with meat mixture. Dampen outer edge with water. Cover with pastry. Press edges to seal. Cut several slits in top crust. Bake in 375°F (190°C) oven for 1 hour until browned. Cut into wedges to serve. Serve hot to 8 hungry people.

1. Stroganoff Meatballs page 106
2. Herb Bread page 128

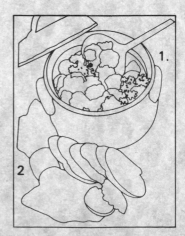

A meat and dumpling dish with a difference.

Cooking oil	3 tbsp.	45 mL
Veal steak cut in squares	2 lbs.	1 kg
Ham slice cut in squares	1 lb.	500 g
All-purpose flour	2 tbsp.	30 mL
Dry mustard	1 tsp.	5 mL
Medium onions, sliced	4	4
Tomato juice	3 cups	700 mL
Lemon juice	1 tbsp.	15 mL
Parsley flakes	2 tbsp.	30 mL
Salt	1 tsp.	5 mL
Pepper	¼ tsp.	1 mL

Heat oil in frying pan. Cut meat into 2-inch (5 cm) squares. Mix flour with mustard. Shake with meat in bag to coat. Brown meat in hot oil.

Add onions and continue to fry. Remove to extra large saucepan. Pour in tomato juice, lemon juice, parsley, salt and pepper. Bring to boil. Simmer 40 minutes. Pour into large casserole. Cover with Tomato Biscuit Crust

TOMATO BISCUIT CRUST

All-purpose flour	2 cups	500 mL
Baking powder	4 tsp.	25 mL
Salt	¾ tsp.	5 mL
Butter or margarine	4 tbsp.	65 mL
Tomato juice	¾ cup	200 mL

Combine flour, baking powder and salt in bowl. Add butter and cut in until crumbly.

Add tomato juice. Stir with fork. Pat out to fit casserole to edges. Bake in 450ºF (230ºC) oven for 20 minutes until browned. Serves 8.

SPAGHETTI SAUCE

Very versatile. While usually served over or with spaghetti, it is equally good as a meat dish with potatoes or rice.

Ground beef	1½ lbs.	700 g
Envelope spaghetti sauce mix	1½ oz.	43 g
Tomato paste	5½ oz.	156 mL
Mushroom pieces and juice	10 oz.	284 mL
Canned tomatoes	19 oz.	540 mL
Medium onion, sliced	1	1
Garlic salt	¼ tsp.	1 mL
Salt	½ tsp.	2 mL
Pepper	¼ tsp.	1 mL

Scramble fry beef in frying pan until brown. Transfer to large pot.

Add rest of ingredients. Stir. Bring to boil. Simmer about 1 hour. Makes enough for ½ lb. (500 g) spaghetti. Serves 8.

BEEF MARGUERITE

Delightfully different. Allow extra time to prepare.

Cooking oil	1 tbsp.	15 mL
Ground beef	1 lb.	500 g
Finely chopped onion	1 cup	250 mL
Ketchup	¼ cup	50 mL
Pepper	¼ tsp.	1 mL
Condensed cream of mushroom soup	¾ cup	175 mL

(continued on next page)

All-purpose flour	2 cups	500 mL
Yellow corn meal	¾ cup	175 mL
Baking powder	2 tbsp.	35 mL
Salt	½ tsp.	3 mL
Curry powder	1 tsp.	5 mL
Shortening	⅓ cup	75 mL
Milk	¾ cup	200 mL

Heat oil in frying pan. Add beef and onion. Brown. Transfer to bowl.

Add ketchup, pepper and soup. Stir. Cool.

In medium-sized bowl, measure in flour, corn meal, baking powder, salt and curry. Stir.

Add shortening. Cut in until crumbly.

Stir in milk. Add more if necessary. Dough should be rather stiff. Turn out on floured board. Knead 10-12 times. Roll out to form 12-inch (30 cm) square. Spread with meat. Roll in jelly roll fashion. Seal seam. Cut into 8 slices. Place in greased pan cut side flat down. Bake in 400°F (200°C) oven for 20-25 minutes. Serve with mushroom sauce. Serves 4-8.

Pictured on page 45.

MUSHROOM SAUCE

Condensed cream of mushroom soup	10 oz.	284 mL
Water	½ cup	125 mL

Heat together in saucepan. Adjust amount of water to acquire desired sauce thickness.

BBQ PORK CHOPS

This is such a good way to serve pork chops. It will wait in the refrigerator until you are ready to bake it.

Pork chops	12	12
Medium onions, cut in slices and separated into rings	3	3
Tomato juice	2 cups	450 mL
Vinegar	2 tbsp.	30 mL
Dry mustard	1 tsp.	5 mL
Worcestershire sauce	1 tbsp.	15 mL
Finely chopped onion	½ cup	125 mL
Chili powder	½ tsp.	2 mL
Salt	½ tsp.	2 mL
Pepper	dash	dash

Brown chops on both sides. Arrange in roaster or large casserole, covering each chop with sliced onion rings.

SAUCE
Combine all sauce ingredients together in medium-sized saucepan. Bring to boil. Simmer slowly for 10 minutes. Pour over chops in roaster. Cover. Bake in 350°F (180°C) oven for 30 minutes. Remove cover and bake for 15 minutes more. Serves 6 people 2 chops each.

Pictured on page 63.

Paré Pointer

His chicken house is so well protected that anyone found near it at night will be found there the next morning.

Easier to make than you think. Really tasty.

Manicotti shells	8	8
Cottage cheese	2 cups	450 g
Eggs	2	2
Parmesan cheese, grated	½ cup	125 mL
Parsley flakes	1 tbsp.	15 mL
Salt	½ tsp.	2 mL
Pepper	⅛ tsp.	½ mL
Minced onion	1 tbsp.	15 mL
Cooking oil	2 tbsp.	30 mL
Ground beef	1 lb.	500 g
Finely chopped onions	½ cup	125 mL
Garlic powder (or 1 clove minced)	¼ tsp.	1 mL
Salt	½ tsp.	2 mL
Tomato sauce	2 — 7½ oz.	2 — 213 mL
Grated Parmesan cheese	2 tbsp.	30 mL

Cook manicotti as directed on package. Rinse with cold water. Drain.

In medium-sized bowl combine cottage cheese, eggs and Parmesan cheese. Stir together well. Add parsley, salt, pepper and onion. Stir well. Using teaspoon, stuff shells. Set aside.

Heat oil in frying pan. Add beef, onions, garlic and salt. Scramble fry until brown. Remove from heat. Stir in tomato sauce. Pour half of meat sauce into 9 x 12-inch (23 x 30 cm) pan. Arrange manicotti over top. Spoon second half of meat sauce over shells.

Sprinkle with Parmesan. Bake uncovered in 350°F (180°C) oven for 45 minutes. Serves 4, 2 shells each.

SAUCY HAM CASSEROLE

A different way to turn out ham. It uses up leftovers too.

Ground ham	4 cups	900 mL
Bread crumbs	1 cup	250 mL
Water	1 cup	250 mL
Dry celery flakes	1 tsp.	5 mL
Dry onion flakes	1 tbsp.	15 mL
All-purpose flour	1 tbsp.	15 mL
Eggs, beaten	2	2
Packed brown sugar	¾ cup	175 mL
All-purpose flour	2 tbsp.	30 mL
Vinegar	¼ cup	50 mL
Salt	¼ tsp.	1 mL
Prepared mustard	2 tbsp.	30 mL
Water	1½ cups	350 mL

Combine ham in large bowl with next 6 ingredients. Mix well. Pat in a 9 x 13-inch (23 x 36 cm) pan. Cover with sauce.

SAUCE

Mix sugar and flour together in saucepan. Stir in vinegar, salt and mustard. Stir in water. Bring to boil over medium heat stirring until thickened. Spread over ham. Bake in 350°F (180°C) oven for 20 minutes or until bubbly and heated through. Cut into 8 servings or into 20 if used as a second meat dish. This can be packed thicker in a smaller-sized pan if desired.

STROGANOFF MEATBALLS

Serve elegant meatballs with universal appeal.

Ground beef	2 lbs.	1 kg
Bread crumbs	1 cup	250 mL
Water	1 cup	250 mL

(continued on next page)

Salt	2 tsp.	10 mL
Pepper	½ tsp.	2 mL
Water	2 cups	450 mL
Small onion, finely chopped	1	1
Instant beef in a mug soup powder	¼ cup	50 mL
Salt	1 tsp.	5 mL
Pepper	¼ tsp.	1 mL
Cornstarch	4 tbsp.	50 mL
Water	¼ cup	50 mL
Sliced mushrooms	10 oz.	284 mL
Condensed cream of mushroom soup	10 oz.	284 mL
Dry parsley flakes	2 tsp.	10 mL
Paprika	¼ tsp.	2 mL
Sour cream	2 cups	500 mL

In large bowl mix beef, crumbs, water, salt and pepper. Shape into about 40 meatballs. Put on cookie sheet with sides. Bake in 425ºF (220ºC) oven for 15 minutes. Pile into casserole.

In medium saucepan put water, onion, soup powder, salt and pepper. Bring to boil.

In small bowl, stir cornstarch into water. Pour into boiling liquid stirring until thickened.

Stir in mushrooms, soup, parsley, paprika and sour cream. If too thick stir in a bit of water.

Pour over meatballs. Cover. Bake in 350ºF (180ºC) oven for 25-30 minutes until heated through. Serves 6.

Pictured on page 99.

CHUCKWAGON CHILI

So easy, top-of-the-stove, doubles well, freezes well, and mild enough for anyone.

Ground beef	1½ lbs.	700 g
Medium onion, chopped	1	1
Kidney beans and juice	14 oz.	398 mL
Mushrooms and juice	10 oz.	284 mL
Wieners, cut in ¼-inch (1 cm) slices	6	6
Medium carrots, sliced	2	2
Condensed tomato soup	10 oz.	284 mL
Salt	1 tsp.	5 mL
Pepper	¼ tsp.	1 mL
Chili powder	1 tsp.	5 mL

Brown beef in frying pan. Remove to large saucepan.

Add rest of ingredients. Stir and bring to boil. Let simmer, covered for an hour or so. Add water if it appears too dry and thick. Taste and add more chili if you so desire. Serves 8.

Pictured on page 9.

SLOPPY JOES

This is one of the easiest dishes to have in the freezer. It takes minutes to heat.

Cooking oil	2 tbsp.	30 mL
Ground beef	2 lbs.	1 kg
Medium onions, chopped	2	2
All-purpose flour	3 tbsp.	45 mL

(continued on next page)

Condensed tomato soup	10 oz.	284 mL
Water, soup can full	2 — 10 oz.	2 — 284 mL
Sugar	1 tbsp.	15 mL
Salt	1½ tsp.	7 mL
Pepper	¼ tsp.	1 mL
Monosodium glutamate	1 tsp.	5 mL

Hamburger buns

Heat oil in frying pan. Add beef and onions. Scramble fry until brown. Sprinkle flour over top. Stir.

Add soup and water stirring until boiling. Add sugar, salt, pepper and monosodium glutamate. Add more water if necessary to thin a bit. Spoon over toasted buns.

SOUPER SUPPER

Brightens up your table with each colorful ingredient showing through.

Condensed cream of mushroom soup	10 oz.	284 mL
Soup can of water	10 oz.	284 ml
Soup can of minute rice	10 oz.	284 mL
Chopped cooked broccoli	1½ cups	350 mL
Cheese slices, cut up	4	4
Ham, cooked and cut up	1½ cups	350 mL

Put soup, water and rice into casserole. Mix together.

Add broccoli, cheese pieces and ham. Stir to distribute evenly. Cover. Bake in 350°F (180°C) oven for 30 minutes. Serves 6.

LASAGNE

No precooking of noodles. Whether served for a meal or a sumptuous late night snack, this is one of the best freezer foods to have on hand.

Ground beef	1 lb.	500 g
Canned tomatoes	2 — 28 oz.	2 — 796 mL
Tomato sauce	7½ oz.	213 mL
Garlic salt	¼ tsp.	1 mL
Envelope spaghetti sauce mix	1½ oz.	42.5 g
Cottage cheese	1 cup	250 g
Egg	1	1
Grated Parmesan cheese	½ cup	125 mL
Mozzarella cheese, shredded	6 oz.	170 g
Wide lasagne noodles, raw	8 oz.	225 g

Brown beef in frying pan. Break up any lumps.

Add tomatoes, sauce, garlic and spaghetti sauce mix. Bring to boil and simmer slowly for 10 minutes. Put some of this on bottom of 9 x 13-inch (22 x 33 cm) pan — just enough to keep noodles from resting on bottom of pan.

In small mixing bowl mix cottage cheese, egg and Parmesan together well.

Assemble:
1. Bit of meat sauce
2. Layer of raw noodles
3. One-third of meat sauce
4. Half of cottage cheese mixture
5. Layer of raw noodles.
6. One-third of meat sauce
7. One-half cottage cheese mixture
8. One-third of meat sauce
9. All mozzarella cheese

(continued on next page)

Cover tightly with foil. Bake in 350ºF (180ºC) oven for 1 hour or more until noodles are tender. Let stand 10 minutes before serving. Serves 8 generously or 12 average.

SPAGHETTI MILD

A good flavored dairy-type casserole without a strong tomato taste.

Spaghetti	7 oz.	198 g
Cooking oil	1 tbsp.	15 mL
Ground beef	1½ lbs.	750 g
Salt	1 tsp.	5 mL
Pepper	¼ tsp.	1 mL
Tomato sauce	2 − 7½ oz.	2 − 213 mL
Chopped green onion	¼ cup	50 mL
Cream cheese	8 oz.	250 g
Cottage cheese	2 cups	500 g
Sour cream	½ cup	125 mL

Cook spaghetti as directed on package. Drain. Put half in 2-quart (2.5L) casserole.

MEAT SAUCE
Brown beef in oil. Drain off fat. Discard.

Add salt, pepper, tomato sauce and onions. Set aside.

CHEESE LAYER
In medium bowl put cream cheese, cottage cheese and sour cream. Stir together well. Put over spaghetti in casserole. Cover with second half of spaghetti. Spoon meat mixture over top. Bake in 350ºF (180ºC) oven for 45 minutes. Serves 8.

SWISS STEW

A good take along dish anytime, anywhere.

Cooking oil	2 tbsp.	30 mL
Round steak	2 lbs.	1 kg
Salt and pepper		
Garlic powder		
Stewed tomatoes	14 oz.	398 mL
Sliced mushrooms with juice	10 oz.	284 mL
Tomato paste	5½ oz.	156 mL
Medium onion, chunked	1	1
Sticks of celery, cut large	4-6	4-6

Cut meat in serving-size pieces. Brown in hot oil in frying pan. Salt and pepper the meat, sprinkle lightly with garlic. Remove to large casserole or small roaster.

In large bowl pour tomatoes, mushrooms and juice and tomato paste. Peel onion and cut into fairly large pieces. Add to tomatoes. Cut celery into 2-inch (5 cm) lengths and add to tomatoes. Stir and pour over meat. Cover. Bake in 350°F (180°C) oven for 2-2½ hours until very tender. Serves 6.

CRISPY MEAT LOAF

Meat with flavor. Appetizing.

Ground beef	1 lb.	500 g
Envelope dry onion soup mix	1½ oz.	42.5 g
Egg	1	1
Warm water	½ cup	125 mL
Ketchup	½ cup	125 mL
Crisp rice cereal	1 cup	250 mL

Combine beef, soup mix, egg, water and ketchup in bowl. Mix together well.

Add cereal to meat and mix in. Pack in 1½-quart (1.5L) casserole. Bake uncovered in 350°F (180°C) oven for 1 hour. Serves 4-6.

An ideal party meal.

Egg, fork beaten	1	1
Water	1 tbsp.	15 mL
Salt	¼ tsp.	1 mL
Pepper	⅛ tsp.	½ mL
Dry bread crumbs (roll to very fine)	½ cup	125 mL
Grated Parmesan cheese	¼ cup	50 mL
Veal cutlets, 4 chops or round steak	1½ lbs.	700 g
Cooking oil	⅓ cup	75 mL
Tomato sauce	7½ oz.	213 mL
Mozzarella cheese slices	4	4

In small bowl combine egg, water, salt and pepper

On large plate mix together crumbs and Parmesan.

Cut in 4 serving pieces. Dip each piece in egg mixture then in crumb mixture. Fry in oil heated in frying pan. Brown both sides. Put in large shallow baking dish.

Pour tomato sauce over top.

Place cheese slice over each piece. Bake covered in 350°F (180°C) oven for 35 minutes until tender. Remove cover. Continue to bake to melt cheese for 10 minutes. Serves 4.

Paré Pointer

It is a known fact that people with bad coughs go to the movies — not the doctor.

TOAD-IN-THE-HOLE

Not a good make ahead. Yorkshire type base. A fun dish.

Sausage links	24	24
Sausage fat	2 tbsp.	30 mL
All-purpose flour	1 cup	250 mL
Salt	¼ tsp.	1 mL
Eggs	2	2
Milk	1 cup	250 mL

Brown sausages in frying pan. Cut in half. Put fat in bottom of 9 x 13-inch (22 x 33 cm) pan. Arrange sausages over bottom. Put in 450°F (230°C) oven while making batter so both fat and sausage will be sizzling hot.

Put flour, salt, eggs and milk in medium bowl. Beat until smooth. Pour over sausages in pan. Bake in 450°F (230°C) oven for 20 minutes. Serves 6.

POT ROAST RAVES

This economical dish will please any company. Gravy will be made at the same time.

Beef roast	3 lbs.	1.3 kg
Envelope dry onion soup mix	1½ oz.	42.5 g
Condensed cream of mushroom soup	10 oz.	284 mL
Medium potatoes	4-6	4-6
Medium carrots	4-6	4-6
Celery sticks	4-6	4-6

On large piece of foil in roaster, put roast. Sprinkle with onion soup mix. Spoon mushroom soup over top. Gather up edges of foil to seal. Cover. Bake in 300°F (150°C) oven for 2½ hours.

Peel potatoes and carrots. Cut celery sticks into 3 pieces each. Open foil. Place vegetables around meat. Reseal. Cover. Bake in 325°F (160°C) oven for 1½ hours. Serves 4-6.

Can easily be adjusted to any amount of guests. There are no extra pans to clean up. A treat in work and eating.

Pot roast	4 lbs.	1.8 kg
Medium potatoes	8-10	8-10
Medium onions, quartered	4	4
Medium carrots, halved	8	8
Medium parsnips, halved	8	8

Put meat in large roaster. If there is hardly any fat showing, pour ¼ cup (50 mL) cooking oil over top of meat. Add more later if needed. Cover. Bake in 300ºF (150ºC) oven for 4 hours.

Peel potatoes. Peel and cut onions in quarters. Peel carrots. Cut in half lengthwise. Peel parsnips and halve lengthwise. Pile vegetables around meat. Sprinkle salt and pepper or not. Good either way. If very dry, add more oil over meat and 1 cup water. Cover. Bake in 325ºF (160ºC) oven for 1 ½ hours. Serves 8.

GRAVY

Drippings left in roaster		
All-purpose flour	6 tbsp.	100 mL
Butter or margarine as needed	1-6 tbsp.	15-100 mL
Salt	¾ tsp.	3 mL
Pepper	¼ tsp.	1 mL
Water	4 cups	900 mL
Gravy browning sauce as needed		

Remove meat and vegetables. Cover. Keep warm. Stir flour into drippings. If not enough drippings, add as much butter as needed to mix flour. Stir in salt and pepper. Add water. Cook and stir until boiling. Add a bit of gravy browning sauce if needed. Taste and add salt if necessary. If gravy is too thick, add water to desired consistency.

Pictured on page 117.

CURRIED WIENERS

A nice fruity flavored casserole.

Apricots or peaches, reserve syrup	14 oz.	398 mL
Apricot syrup	½ cup	125 mL
Apricot nectar	10 oz.	284 mL
Curry powder	1 tsp.	5 mL
Cornstarch	2 tbsp.	30 mL
Water	2 tbsp.	30 mL
Wieners, cut in bite-sized pieces	12	12

Put drained apricots in 1½-quart (1.5L) casserole.

In medium saucepan combine apricot syrup and nectar.

Mix cornstarch with water and stir into juice, stirring until thickened. Pour into casserole.

Add cut up wieners. Stir to combine. Bake in 350°F (180°C) oven for 30 minutes until hot and bubbly. Serves 4.

1. Italian Stew page 65
2. Oven Pot Roast page 115

BARBECUED RIBS

A delicious blend of flavors. Worthy of you.

Meaty spareribs	4 lbs.	1.8 kg
Cooking oil	3 tbsp.	45 mL
Large onion, chopped	1	1
Ketchup	1 cup	225 mL
Water	1 cup	225 mL
Vinegar	½ cup	125 mL
Packed brown sugar	½ cup	125 mL
Worcestershire sauce	1 tsp.	5 mL
Salt	1 tsp.	5 mL

Cut ribs into serving pieces. Brown in oil in frying pan or under broiler. Put into large roaster.

In medium-sized bowl combine onion, ketchup, water, vinegar, sugar, Worcestershire and salt. Stir. Pour evenly over ribs. Cover. Bake in 350°F (180°C) oven for 2 hours. Remove cover. Continue to cook for 15 minutes. Serves 6.

QUICK PORK CHOPS

An easy casserole to prepare when time is short.

Pork chops	6-8	6-8
Salt and pepper		
Condensed cream of mushroom soup	10 oz.	284 mL

Brown chops if time permits. Cut off most of the fat if not browning. Layer in large casserole or small roaster. Salt and pepper each chop.

Spoon soup over top without diluting. Cover. Bake in 350°F (180°C) oven 1½ hours until tender. Will take a little longer if not browned first. Serves 4.

SPAGHETTI AND MEATBALLS

Not a quick meal to make but it is all there together when ready. Not a good make ahead.

SAUCE

Cooking oil	1 tbsp.	15 mL
Chopped onion	1 cup	250 mL
Garlic powder (or 1 clove of garlic minced)	¼ tsp.	1 mL
Tomato paste	5½ oz.	156 mL
Canned tomatoes	19 oz.	540 mL
Granulated sugar	2 tbsp.	30 mL
Salt	1 tsp.	5 mL
Pepper	¼ tsp.	1 mL
Oregano	pinch	pinch
Parsley	1 tbsp.	15 mL

Heat oil in frying pan. Sauté onion and garlic until soft.

Add rest of ingredients and simmer slowly 1 hour or so.

MEATBALLS

Ground beef	1 lb.	500 g
Bread crumbs	½ cup	125 mL
Dry onion flakes	1 tsp.	5 mL
Water	⅓ cup	75 mL
Salt	1 tsp.	5 mL
Pepper	¼ tsp.	1 mL

Mix all ingredients together. Shape in 20 small meatballs. Brown well.

Spaghetti	7 oz.	198 g
Parmesan cheese	2 tbsp.	30 mL

Prepare spaghetti according to package directions. Put in large flared serving bowl or platter. Add meatballs. Pour sauce over top. Sprinkle with Parmesan cheese. Serves 4.

A tasty way to serve lamb. Refreshing change.

Butter or margarine	¼ cup	50 mL
Chopped onions	1½ cups	450 mL
Garlic clove, minced (optional)	1	1
Lamb stew meat, cubed	2 lbs.	1 kg
All-purpose flour	2 tbsp.	30 mL
Butter or margarine	2 tbsp.	30 mL
Granulated Sugar	1 tsp.	5 mL
Salt	1 tsp.	5 mL
Curry powder	2-3 tsp.	10-15 mL
Beef bouillon cubes	2	2
Water	2 cups	500 mL
Sour cream or thick cream	½ cup	125 mL

Melt butter in frying pan. Add onions and garlic. Sauté until soft. Transfer to 2½-quart (3L) casserole.

Put stew meat in frying pan. Brown well. Pile over onions.

Stir flour and butter into frying pan. Add sugar, salt, curry, bouillon cubes and water. Stir until thickened and cubes are dissolved. Adjust curry now if you want more. Pour over meat. Stir to combine. Cover. Bake in 350°F (180°C) oven for 1½-2 hours until tender.

Stir in cream. Ready to serve 8.

RUEBEN CASSEROLE

So you think you don't like sauerkraut? Try this.

Jar of sauerkraut	28 oz.	796 mL
Butter or margarine	2 tbsp.	30 mL
Chopped onion	½ cup	125 mL
Corned beef, cut up	12 oz.	340 mL
Russian dressing	¾ cup	175 mL
Swiss cheese slices	4	4

Drain sauerkraut. Rinse well. Drain. Put in 2½-quart (3L) casserole.

Heat butter in medium saucepan. Sauté onions until soft.

Add corned beef and dressing to onions. Stir together. Spoon over sauerkraut.

Layer cheese over top. Bake uncovered in 350ºF (180ºC) oven for 30 minutes until heated through. Serves 4.

Serve with rye bread.

CHINESE PEPPER STEAK

One of the easiest versions, yet oh so good.

Cooking oil	3 tbsp.	45 mL
Round steak cut in ½-inch (2 cm) strips	2 lbs.	1 kg
Flour to coat	¼ cup	50 mL
Salt	½ tsp.	2 mL
Pepper	⅛ tsp.	0.5 mL

(continued on next page)

Green peppers, seeded and thinly sliced	3	3
Medium onions, thinly sliced	2	2
Garlic clove, minced	1	1
Tomato sauce	7½ oz.	213 mL
Soy sauce	¼ cup	50 mL
Beef bouillon cube	1	1
Water	¼ cup	50 mL
Whole mushrooms and juice	10 oz.	284 mL

Heat oil in frying pan. Cut meat into short strips. Put in paper or plastic bag containing flour, salt and pepper. Shake to coat. Brown. Transfer to 2½-quart (3L) casserole.

Put peppers, onions and garlic in pan. Sauté until soft.

Add tomato and soy sauce, beef cube, water, mushrooms and juice. Break up and dissolve cube. Pour over meat. Cover. Bake in 350°F (180°C) oven for 1 hour or more until very tender. Serves 8.

QUICK MEAT LOAF

A real man pleaser.

Bread crumbs	1 cup	250 mL
Envelope dry onion soup mix	1½ oz.	42.5 g
Ketchup	¾ cup	175 mL
Water	½ cup	125 mL
Eggs	2	2
Salt	2 tsp.	10 mL
Pepper	½ tsp.	2 mL
Ground beef	2 lbs.	1 kg
Grated Cheddar cheese (optional)	1 cup	250 mL

Put first 7 ingredients into bowl. Mix well.

Add beef and combine well. Pack into 2-quart (2L) casserole. Bake uncovered in 350°F (180°C) oven for 1¼-1½ hours. Sprinkle with cheese and put back in oven long enough to melt. Serves 6-8.

MEAT LOAF CLASSIC

Nice and moist, a winning mixture.

Ground beef	1½ lbs.	700 g
Beaten egg	1	1
Milk	¾ cup	175 mL
Rolled oats	¾ cup	175 mL
Instant onion flakes	1 tbsp.	15 mL
Parsley flakes	1 tsp.	5 mL
Worcestershire sauce	1 tsp.	5 mL
Salt	1½ tsp.	7 mL
Pepper	¼ tsp.	1 mL
Grated Cheddar cheese	1 cup	250 mL
Ketchup	4 tbsp.	50 mL

Put first 9 ingredients into large bowl. Mix together well. Pack half into loaf pan 9 x 5 x 3-inches (23 x 12 x 7 cm).

Spread grated cheese over meat.

Put second half of meat mixture over cheese. Flatten top.

Spread ketchup over top of loaf.

Bake uncovered in 350ºF (180ºC) oven for 1¼-1½ hours. Serves 6-8.

BEEF PIE

This is not a stew but rather a main dish. Made up in small pie plates there can be nothing handier to have on hand.

Cooking oil	2 tbsp.	30 mL
Blade steak	4½ lbs.	2 kg
Onion, quartered	1	1
Celery stick, cut up	1	1
Carrot, cut up	1	1

(continued on next page)

124

Water	6 cups	1.4 L
Salt	1 tsp.	5 mL
Pepper	¼ tsp.	1 mL
Cornstarch	3 tbsp.	45 mL
Water	3 tbsp.	45 mL

Pie crust, your own or a mix.
  See page 127.

Brown steaks on both sides in hot oil. Transfer to roaster.

Add onion, celery and carrot pieces.

Pour water, salt and pepper into frying pan. Stir to loosen all bits stuck to pan. Bring to boil. Mix cornstarch with water. Stir into boiling water stirring until it boils again. Pour over meat and vegetables. Cover. Bake in 325ºF (160ºC) oven for 2-2½ hours until very tender. Remove steaks to cutting board. Cut meat into small pieces. There will be about 5 cups. Strain gravy. You will need 3 cups of not too thick consistency.

Line 8 foil pot pie pans 4⅜ x 1⅜ inches (11.1 x 3.5 cm) with pastry.

Divide meat among pans. Pour ⅓ cup gravy over each. Dampen edges. Cover with top crust and seal. Cut vents in top crust. Bake in lower third of 400ºF (200ºC) oven for 30 minutes until top pastry is dry and browned nicely. Allow 1 pie per serving.

Pictured on page 135.

Paré Pointer

After you hear several eye-witness accounts of an accident, you begin to wonder about history.

GRAHAM MEAT LOAF

The added wafer crumbs give a faint sweetish flavor to this good loaf.

Graham cracker crumbs	⅔ cup	150 mL
Milk	⅔ cup	150 mL
Ketchup	¼ cup	50 mL
Chopped onion	⅓ cup	75 mL
Eggs	2	2
Salt	1 tsp.	5 mL
Pepper	¼ tsp.	1 mL
Ground beef	1 lb.	500 g

Ketchup for drizzle

Put first 7 ingredients in medium-sized bowl. Mix together well.

Add meat and mix well. Pack into small loaf pan.

Drizzle ketchup over top. Bake uncovered in 350ºF (180ºC) oven for 1 hour. Serves 4.

BAKING POWDER BISCUITS

Simple to make with soft crust or crisp.

All-purpose flour	2 cups	450 mL
Baking powder, double action	4 tsp.	20 mL
Granulated Sugar	1 tbsp.	15 mL
Salt	¾ tsp.	3 mL
Butter, margarine or shortening or lard	4 tbsp.	60 mL
Milk	⅞ cup	200 mL

Measure dry ingredients into medium bowl.

(continued on next page)

Add butter. Cut into flour mixture until crumbly.

Add milk. Stir with fork until gathered and mixed. Turn out on lightly floured board. Knead gently 10 times. Roll or pat dough out to ¾ inch (2 cm) thick. Cut with round 2-inch (5 cm) cookie cutter. If cut in squares, no re-cutting is necessary. Put on ungreased baking sheet; close together for soft sides, 1 inch (2.5 cm) apart for crisp sides. Bake in 450°F (230°C) oven for 12-15 minutes until browned. These brown nicely if you brush tops lightly with milk before baking.

Pictured on page 27.

PIE CRUST PASTRY

For quiches, meat pies or as a covering for casseroles.

All-purpose flour	5 cups	1.1 L
Salt	2 tsp.	10 mL
Baking powder	1 tsp.	5 mL
Brown sugar	3 tbsp.	45 mL
Lard, room temperature	1 lb	454 g
Egg	1	1
Vinegar	2 tbsp.	30 mL
Add cold water to make	1 cup	225 mL

Measure flour, salt, baking powder and brown sugar into large bowl. Stir together to distribute all ingredients.

Add lard. Cut into pieces with knife. With pastry cutter, cut in lard until whole mixture is crumbly and feels moist.

Break egg into measuring cup. Fork beat well. Add vinegar. Pour cold water to measure 1 cup (225 mL). Pour slowly over flour mixture stirring with fork to distribute. With hands, work until it will hold together. Divide into 4 equal parts. Each part is sufficient for a 2-crust pie. Wrap in plastic and store in refrigerator for 1 or 2 weeks. Store in freezer to have a continuing supply.

MUSTARD BEANS

A yummy sauce and keeps well too.

Packed brown sugar	½ cup	125 mL
Granulated sugar	½ cup	125 mL
All-purpose flour	6 tbsp.	100 mL
Dry mustard	1 tbsp.	15 mL
Turmeric	1 tsp.	5 mL
Celery seed	¼ tsp.	1 mL
Vinegar	1½ cups	375 mL
Water	1½ cups	375 mL
Cut wax beans, drained	3 - 14 oz.	3 - 398 mL

Combine all dry ingredients in medium-sized saucepan. Mix together very well.

Add vinegar and water. Stir over medium high heat until boiling.

Add beans. Stir lightly. Pour into container. Cover. Store in refrigerator for 1 or 2 days before eating. it is best to use a glass jar. A plastic bowl will stain.

Pictured on page 45.

HERB BREAD

A hint of this, a hint of that. Easy to increase for spicier appetites.

French bread loaf	1	1
Butter	½ cup	125 mL
Garlic powder	⅛ tsp.	0.5 mL
Sage	⅛ tsp.	0.5 mL

(continued on next page)

Parsley flakes	¼ tsp.	1 mL
Basil	⅛ tsp.	0.5 mL
Oregano	⅛ tsp.	0.5 mL
Celery salt	⅛ tsp.	0.5 mL

Slice into thick slices.

Cream butter, garlic, sage, parsley, basil, oregano and celery salt in medium-sized bowl. Spread on each slice. Put together in original shape. Wrap in foil. Heat in 350°F (180°C) oven for 20-25 minutes. If time is short, slices can be arranged on baking sheet and broiled. Watch carefully as they burn easily.

Pictured on page 99.

FRUIT COMPOTE

Gives an elegant look to any buffet. Tastes every bit as good as it looks.

Canned peaches with juice	14 oz.	398 mL
Canned pears with juice	14 oz.	398 mL
Canned pineapple tidbits with juice	14 oz.	398 mL
Canned orange segments, drained	12 oz.	341 mL
Maraschino cherries, drained	20-24	20-24
Packed brown sugar	¾ cup	175 mL
Curry powder	1 tsp.	5 mL
Cornstarch	3 tbsp.	45 mL
Water	¼ cup	50 mL

Slice peaches and pears. Put all fruit in medium-sized saucepan. Add sugar and curry. Bring to boil.

Mix cornstarch into water. Pour into boiling fruit stirring constantly until boiling again and thickened. Pour into casserole. Cover. Hold in warm oven or reheat in 350°F (180°C) oven for 30 minutes until bubbly hot. Serves 12.

CHOW CHOW

An old-time recipe especially good with roasted meat served with gravy — beef, pork, chicken, turkey. Makes a large enough batch to allow giving some away.

Onions, sliced	5 lbs.	3.2 kg
Green tomatoes, very firm, sliced	16 lbs.	7.2 kg
Salt	1 cup	250 mL
Granulated sugar	5 lbs.	2.2 kg
Pickling spice in bag	3 oz.	85 g
Turmeric	2 tbsp.	30 mL
Vinegar	2 quarts	2 L

Peel onions. Slice in ¼ inch (½ cm) slices. Cut up slices. Remove stem end from tomatoes. Slice in ¼ inch (½ cm) slices. Cut up slices. Slicing tomatoes after onions will remove onion smell from hands. Layer tomatoes, onions and salt in large, heavy preserving kettle. Cover. Let stand overnight.

Next day drain well. Add sugar. Secure pickling spice in bag made of any clean fabric — unbleached cotton is good. Push bag down among tomatoes. Add turmeric. Pour on vinegar until it is barely visible around edges. Too much vinegar will make too much juice. Bring to boil, stirring frequently. Simmer about 2 hours. Remove spice bag and discard. Adjust sugar now. Go by taste. Add more if not sweet enough. Add more turmeric if needed to make a pleasing color. Pour into clean, sterilized jars. Seal. Yield: 9-10 quarts or the equivalent in small jars.

Note: Do not use enamel container to make Chow Chow as it will scorch on the bottom.

Pictured on page 63.

Here's an old classic from way back. It is still good.

Canned tomatoes	28 oz.	796 mL
Granulated sugar	1 tsp.	5 mL
Finely chopped onion	¼ cup	50 mL
Finely chopped celery	2 tbsp.	30 mL
Water	½ cup	125 mL
Salt	½ tsp.	2 mL
All-purpose flour	1 cup	250 mL
Baking powder	2 tsp.	10 mL
Sugar	1 tsp.	5 mL
Salt	½ tsp.	2 mL
Shortening	1 tbsp.	15 mL
Milk	½ cup	125 mL

In large pot combine tomatoes, sugar, onion, celery, water and salt. Bring to boil.

In medium-sized bowl combine flour, baking powder, sugar and salt. Cut in shortening until crumbly. Add milk. Stir to mix. Drop by spoonfuls over boiling tomatoes. Cover. Keep boiling without removing lid for 15 minutes. Serves 6.

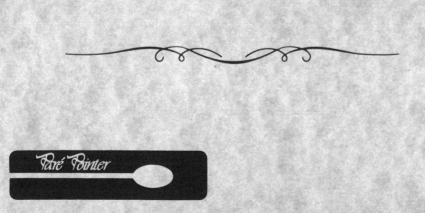

Paré Pointer

As you travel around you will notice that traffic is like ketchup in a bottle. First none comes, then a lot'll.

VEGETABLE SUPREME

A good do-ahead vegetable.

Small cauliflower, broken up	1	1
Frozen baby carrots	10 oz.	283 g
Frozen Brussels sprouts	10 oz.	283 g
Button mushrooms, drained	10 oz.	283 g
Condensed cream of celery soup	10 oz.	284 mL
Condensed cream of Cheddar soup	10 oz.	284 mL
Milk	⅓ cup	75 mL
Parsley flakes	1 tsp.	5 mL

Break cauliflower up into flowerets in large saucepan.

Add carrots and sprouts. Add enough water to parboil until not quite cooked. Drain. Place in 2-quart (2L) casserole.

Add mushrooms to vegetables.

In medium-sized dish, stir celery soup, Cheddar soup, milk and parsley together well. Pour over vegetables. Stir lightly. Bake uncovered in 400°F (200°C) oven for 35 minutes. Serves 6-8.

BAKED BEANS

So easy and quick. Barbecue maybe. Or just an extra.

Beans in tomato sauce	3 — 14 oz.	3 — 398 mL
Packed brown sugar	¼ cup	50 mL
Ketchup	1 cup	225 mL
Large onion, chopped	¾ cup	175 mL
Worcestershire sauce	1½ tsp.	7 mL

Put all ingredients in 3-quart (4L) casserole. Stir to combine. Bake uncovered in 350°F (180°C) oven for 1½ hours or until bubbling throughout and well browned around edges.

Serves 8-10.

Try a change from just plain corn. A favorite.

Eggs	2	2
Creamed corn	14 oz.	398 mL
All-purpose flour	2 tbsp.	30 mL
Granulated sugar	1 tbsp.	15 mL
Butter or margarine	1 tbsp.	15 mL
Milk	¾ cup	175 mL
Salt	1 tsp.	5 mL
Pepper	⅛ tsp.	0.5 mL
Dry onion flakes	1 tsp.	5 mL
Butter or margarine	1 tbsp.	15 mL
Bread crumbs	½ cup	125 mL

Break eggs into medium-sized bowl. Beat with a spoon to mix. Add corn, flour, sugar and butter. Mix together well until flour is blended.

Add milk, salt, pepper and onion. Mix and pour into 1-quart (1L) casserole.

Melt butter in small saucepan. Stir in crumbs. Sprinkle over corn. Bake in 350ºF (180ºC) oven for about 1 hour or until set and crumbs have browned. Serves 4-6.

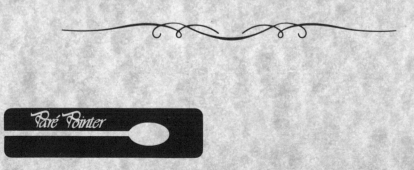

Paré Pointer

Marriages are made in heaven so go ahead and harp at each other.

BAKED BEANS AND PINEAPPLE

Everyday beans dressed up for company.

Cooking oil	1 tbsp.	15 mL
Chopped onions	1 cup	250 mL
Deep browned beans in tomato sauce	19 oz.	540 mL
Red kidney beans	14 oz.	398 mL
Crushed pineapple	1 cup	250 mL
Ketchup	⅓ cup	75 mL
Prepared mustard	1 tsp.	5 mL
Packed brown sugar	½ cup	125 mL
Instant bacon bits	1 tbsp.	15 mL
Worcestershire sauce	¼ tsp.	1 mL
Salt	¼ tsp.	1 mL
Pepper	⅛ tsp.	½ mL

Heat oil in pan. Add onions and sauté slowly until limp. Put in 1½-quart (1.5L) casserole.

Add remaining ingredients in order given. Stir to mix. Bake uncovered in 350ºF (180ºC) oven for 1½ hours until bubbly. Stir once or twice during baking. Serves 6-8.

1. Moussaka page 94
2. Beef Pie page 124

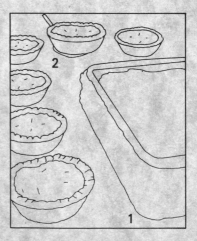

MACARONI AND CHEESE

A creamy, cheesy casserole that you can adapt to cheese lovers simply by adding more cheese to the sauce.

Macaroni, raw	2 cups	500 mL
Butter or margarine	4 tbsp.	50 mL
Dry onion flakes	1 tbsp.	15 mL
All-purpose flour	3 tbsp.	50 mL
Salt	½ tsp.	2 mL
Pepper	⅛ tsp.	0.5 mL
Milk	2 cups	500 mL
Shredded cheese	1 cup	250 mL
Butter or margarine	1 tbsp.	15 mL
Bread crumbs	½ cup	125 mL
Shredded cheese	¼ cup	50 mL

Cook macaroni as directed on package. Drain. Set aside.

In medium-sized saucepan, melt butter. Stir in onions, flour, salt and pepper. Add milk. Cook and stir until sauce boils and thickens. Add cheese. Stir to melt. Combine with macaroni. Pour into 2-quart (2L) casserole.

In small saucepan, melt butter. Remove from heat. Stir in crumbs until coated. Add cheese, stirring to distribute. Sprinkle over top. Bake in 350°F (180°C) oven for 30 minutes until hot and bubbly and cheese is melted. Serves 4-6.

SCALLOPED POTATOES

With this method you never find little lumps of flour among the potatoes.

Butter or margarine	4 tbsp.	60 mL
All-purpose flour	4 tbsp.	60 mL
Salt	1½ tsp.	7 mL
Pepper	⅛ tsp.	0.5 mL
Milk	2 cups	500 mL
Medium-sized potatoes	6	6
Large onion, chopped or sliced thinly into rings	1	1

In medium saucepan melt butter. Stir in flour, salt and pepper. Add milk. Stir constantly until boiling. Remove from heat.

Peel potatoes. Slice thinly. Peel onion and chop or if you prefer, slice thinly and separate into rings. Layer half of potatoes and onions in 2-quart (2.5L) casserole. Pour half the sauce over. Layer rest of potatoes and onions on top. Cover with rest of sauce. Bake covered in 350°F (180°C) oven for 50 minutes. Uncover and bake 15 minutes or until potatoes are tender. Serves 6.

FRENCH BEANS AMANDINE

A delicious do ahead vegetable. Easy to multiply.

Frenched green beans, drained	2 — 14 oz.	2 — 398 mL
Condensed cream of mushroom soup	10 oz.	284 mL
Slivered almonds	2 tbsp.	30 mL

(continued on next page)

Put drained beans in a 1½-quart (1.5L) casserole. Spoon soup over top. Lift lightly with a fork to mix. Smooth top. Sprinkle almonds over top. Cover. Heat in 350°F (180°C) oven for 20-30 minutes until hot and bubbly. Use more almonds throughout if you like. Additional nuts may be added to the casserole contents as well. Serves 6-8.

CREAMED CABBAGE BAKE

About the best way to serve cabbage as a vegetable.

Medium cabbage, chopped, cooked	1	1
Finely chopped onion (optional)	½ cup	125 mL
Butter or margarine	3 tbsp.	45 mL
All-purpose flour	3 tbsp.	45 mL
Salt	½ tsp.	2 mL
Pepper	⅛ tsp.	½ mL
Milk	2 cups	450 mL

Grated Cheddar cheese (optional)

Chop cabbage coarsely. Boil in salted water along with onion until tender crisp. Drain. Put in 1½-quart (1½L) casserole.

Melt butter in medium saucepan. Stir in flour, salt and pepper. Add milk. Cook, stirring until sauce boils. Pour over cabbage and onion.

Sprinkle with grated cheese. Bake uncovered in 350°F (180°C) oven for 20-30 minutes until bubbly.

WILD RICE CASSEROLE

A delightfully different vegetable dish to serve.

Long-grain and wild rice mixture	6 oz.	170 g
Broccoli, 2 heads (approx.)	2 lbs.	1 kg
Condensed cream of mushroom soup	2 — 10 oz.	2 — 284 mL
Cheddar cheese, grated	½ lb.	250 g
Cheddar cheese, grated	½ cup	125 mL

Cook rice according to package directions. Put ½ rice in bottom of 2½-quart (3L) casserole.

Boil broccoli until just barely tender crisp. Drain. Put ½ broccoli over rice. Spoon second half of rice over top followed with second half of broccoli.

In large bowl, combine soup and cheese. Spoon over top. Bake uncovered in 350°F (180°C) oven for 50 minutes.

Sprinkle cheese over top and bake 10-15 minutes more. Serves 8.

TOMATO MACARONI AND CHEESE

This variation uses tomatoes instead of milk.

Macaroni, raw	2 cups	500 mL
Canned tomatoes	14 oz.	398 mL
Dry onion flakes	1 tbsp.	15 mL
Sugar	1 tsp.	5 mL
Salt	½ tsp.	2 mL
Pepper	⅛ tsp.	0.5 mL

(continued on next page)

140

Grated Cheddar cheese	1 cup	250 mL

Cook macaroni according to package directions. Drain. Pour into 2-quart (2L) casserole.

In medium-sized bowl, combine tomatoes with onion flakes, sugar, salt and pepper. Pour over macaroni. Stir lightly.

Sprinkle grated cheese over top. Bake uncovered in 350°F (180°C) oven for 30 minutes until hot and cheese is melted. Serves 4-6.

CYNTHIA'S LAZY CABBAGE ROLLS

If you love cabbage rolls but lack the expertise to make them, this is surely second best.

Finely shredded cabbage, packed	4 cups	1 L
Long-grain rice, raw	½ cup	125 mL
Salt	1 tsp.	5 mL
Pepper sprinkle	1	1
Water	1¾ cups	425 mL
Butter or margarine	¼ cup	50 mL
Finely chopped onion	1½ tbsp.	25 mL

Put finely grated cabbage into 1½-quart (1.5L) casserole.

Pour rice over top. Poke fork here and there to allow a bit of rice into the cabbage. Sprinkle salt over rice and a light sprinkle of pepper. Pour water over all. Cover. Bake in 350°F (180°C) oven for 1 hour until rice is cooked and cabbage is tender. Remove from oven. If it seems too dry, add a bit of boiling water. It will absorb.

Heat butter in small frying pan. Add onion and sauté slowly until golden. Add both onions and butter to cabbage. Stir to combine. Serves 4.

GROUP STROGANOFF

Uses stored up leftover cooked beef from your freezer. Practical for large buffets, especially stand-up situations since no knife is needed. Chicken and/or turkey may be substituted for the beef.

Water	10 cups	2.25 L
Dry onion flakes	1 cup	225 mL
Instant beef in a mug soup mix	6 oz.	170 g
Cornstarch	1 cup	225 mL
Water	1 cup	225 mL
Mushroom pieces and juice	4 — 10 oz.	4 — 284 mL
Condensed cream of mushroom soup	4 — 10 oz.	4 — 284 mL
Parsley flakes	2 tbsp.	30 mL
Salt	2 tbsp.	30 mL
Pepper	1 tsp.	5 mL
Paprika	1-2 tbsp.	15-30 mL
Sour cream	8 cups	1.8 L
Cooked roast beef, cut up in bite-sized pieces	10 lbs.	4.5 kg

In large saucepan put water, onion and soup mix. Stir occasionally as you bring it to a boil.

In small bowl, stir cornstarch with water. Add to boiling broth, stirring until boiling again and thickened. Pour into large turkey-sized roaster.

Empty mushrooms, soup, parsley, salt, pepper and paprika into roaster. Add sour cream. Stir together well. Amount of paprika you add depends on color. Add cut up beef. If you don't know how much 10 pounds (4.5 kg.) makes up, fill an ice cream pail and add about 2 of them. Stir to combine. If not too stiff with meat, add a bit more. Bake uncovered in 350ºF (180ºC) oven for 1½-2 hours until hot and bubbly and browning a bit around edges. Serves 40-50 people.

The best midnight meal going! Doubled in size for easy following. Make up two roasters for 50 people.

Large macaroni shells	16 oz.	500 g
Ground beef	4 lbs.	2 kg
Medium onions, chopped	4	4
Garlic powder	½ tsp.	2 mL
Canned stewed tomatoes	2 — 14 oz.	2 — 398 mL
Spaghetti sauce	2 — 14 oz.	2 — 398 mL
Mushroom pieces and juice	2 — 10 oz.	2 — 284 mL
Sour cream	4 cups	1 L
Medium Cheddar cheese	1 lb.	500 g
Mozzarella cheese	1 lb.	500 g

Cook macaroni as directed on package. Rinse with cold water. Drain. Set aside.

Brown beef in frying pan. Transfer to extra large pot. Add onions, garlic, tomatoes, spaghetti sauce, mushrooms and juice. Bring to a boil. Simmer, stirring occasionally for 20 minutes until onions are tender. Remove from heat. Use large turkey-sized roaster to assemble.

Construction.
1. Spread half macaroni over bottom
2. Pour over one-half of meat sauce
3. Spread with one-half sour cream
4. Slice Cheddar cheese thinly and layer half on top
5. Cover with second half of macaroni
6. Spoon over second half of meat sauce
7. Spread with second half of sour cream
8. Cover with second half of Cheddar cheese slices
9. Top with thinly sliced mozzarella cheese

Cover. Bake in 350°F (180°C) oven for about 1 hour 15 minutes or until bubbling hot. Remove cover. If cheese is not melted, continue to bake a few more minutes to melt. Serves 25.

PORK CHOPS IN BBQ SAUCE

Make this a day ahead. You can feed as many people as you have oven space for roasters.

Pork chops	90	90
Medium onions, cut in slices and separated into rings	12	12
Tomato juice	12 cups	3 L
Vinegar	¾ cup	175 mL
Worcestershire sauce	6 tbsp.	100 mL
Dry mustard	2 tbsp.	30 mL
Finely chopped onion	3 cups	700 mL
Chili powder	1 tbsp.	15 mL
Salt	1 tbsp.	15 mL
Pepper	½ tsp.	2 mL

Brown all chops, keeping in mind browning is the main objective, not necessarily cooking them. Layer in 2 large roasters, covering each layer with onion rings.

SAUCE
Combine all sauce ingredients in an extra large saucepan. Bring to boil and allow to simmer uncovered for at least 10 minutes. Pour over chops. Cover. Bake in 350ºF (180ºC) oven for 1½ hours. Remove covers. Continue to bake 20 minutes longer. Serves 45 people, 2 chops each. Allow at least 30 minutes extra time if taken from refrigerator to oven.

If you ever wonder why a rabbit has a shiny nose, it's because its puff is at the other end.

This can be made up well before you need it. Great for family gatherings. Use all white meat or a larger proportion of dark as desired.

Chicken thighs	32	32
Chicken breasts, cut into 3 pieces each	32	32
All-purpose flour	6 cups	1.3 L
Salt	6 tbsp.	100 mL
Pepper	1½ tbsp.	25 mL
Paprika	6 tbsp.	100 mL

Have butcher cut breasts unless you have a cleaver. A small hatchet works well. Put cardboard over breadboard for cutting without gouging.

Combine flour, salt, pepper and paprika in large paper bag (or plastic bag or large container with tight-fitting cover). Put several pieces of chicken in bag. Shake to coat. Place on baking pans. Brown in 450°F (230°C) oven for 20 minutes until brown. Arrange in 2 large roasters when finished browning. If you use broiler, turn to brown both sides.

Bake covered in 350°F (180°C) oven for 1½-2 hours until tender. Allow extra half hour if refrigerated. Serves 50.

Paré Pointer

A sweater is usually put on a child when the mother feels chilly.

BEEF STEW AND DUMPLINGS

There are no potatoes in this stew. They can be served on the side with a green salad and buns for a filling meal.

Stew meat, cut up	20 lbs.	9 kg
Cooking oil for browning		
Salt	6 tbsp.	100 mL
Pepper	1 tbsp.	15 mL
Water		
Frozen sliced carrots (not diced)	8 lbs.	3.6 kg
Large Spanish onions	7	7
Frozen peas	4 lbs.	1.8 kg

Brown meat in oil if time permits. Otherwise add gravy coloring at end of recipe. Put meat in large pot or 2 or 3 smaller pots.

Add salt and pepper. Pour water over meat until you can just see it around the sides. Cover. Bring to boil. Simmer for 1½-2 hours until very tender. May be prepared this far 1 or 2 days ahead. When ready to finish, divide meat and juice among 3 large roasters. Two roasters will hold all of the stew but you get more dumplings using 3. Stir in browning sauce now if needed. Add more water if there isn't enough in each roaster to boil for a few minutes.

Cook carrots as directed on package. Drain. Divide among 3 roasters.

Peel onions and cut in chunks. Add small amount of water and simmer until tender. Drain. Divide among roasters.

Cook peas as directed on package. Drain. Divide among roasters. Stir contents of each roaster lightly to distribute vegetables evenly throughout. Place uncovered in 375ºF (190ºC) oven. Stir occasionally. Heat until bubbling hot. Put dumplings over top and bake as directed.

(continued on next page)

DUMPLINGS

Tea biscuit mix	4 cups	1 L
Milk (as on package)	1½ cup	375 mL
Tea biscuit mix	4 cups	1 L
Milk (as on package)	1½ cups	375 mL
Tea biscuit mix	4 cups	1 L
Milk (as on package)	1½ cups	375 mL

While this can be mixed in 1 bowl, it is much easier to mix in 3 separate amounts for easy dividing. Measure biscuit mix and milk into bowl. Mix lightly with fork. Drop by spoonful over 1 roaster of boiling stew making 24 dumplings. Repeat for other 2 roasters. Bake uncovered in 425°F (220°C) oven for 15 minutes until biscuits are nicely browned. Serves 50.

HOMECOMING BEANS

This dish has been served to many a gathering.

Beans in tomato sauce	14 — 14 oz.	14 — 398 mL
Dry onion flakes	½ cup	125 mL
Packed brown sugar	1 cup	250 mL
Ketchup	4 cups	900 mL
Worcestershire sauce	2 tbsp.	30 mL

Combine all 5 ingredients together in large roaster.

Bake uncovered in 350°F (180°C) oven for 2-2½ hours or until bubbling and darkening around sides. Stir halfway through cooking time. Serves 50.

If you let your cat eat lemons it is apt to become a sourpuss.

SWEET AND SOUR BUTTON BONES

For large groups, the pork button bones give much more meat for the cooking space required than spare ribs. If using spare ribs, you will need more.

Button bones	25 lbs.	11 kg
Water		
Packed brown sugar	8 cups	2 L
Water	8 cups	2 L
Vinegar	4 cups	1 L
Soy sauce	½ cup	100 mL
Cornstarch	1 cup	250 mL
Cold water	1 cup	250 mL

Cut button bones into short lengths for easy handling and serving. Put into 2 large pots. Pour water into each pot about 5 inches (12 cm) deep. Bring to boil. Simmer covered for 1½ hours until tender. Drain and divide between 2 roasters.

Put brown sugar, water, vinegar and soy sauce in large pot. Stir. Bring to boil.

Combine cornstarch and water stirring to blend. Pour into hot mixture stirring until it begins to boil again. Pour half of sauce over each roaster. Cover with foil. Bake in 350ºF (180ºC) oven for 30 minutes or until hot and bubbly. Serves 50.

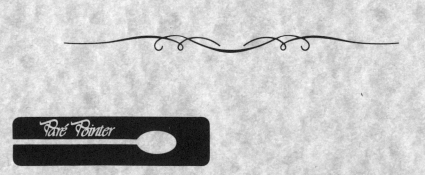

Paré Pointer

Barns wouldn't be so noisy if cows didn't have horns.

PORK CHOP CASSEROLE

Preparation time couldn't be shorter for so many people. Browning can be skipped if need be. Just cut off excessive fat.

Pork chops	90	90
Salt and pepper		
Condensed cream of mushroom soup	10 — 10 oz.	10 — 284 mL

Brown if time permits. A barbeque works well and quickly weather permitting. Layer in 2 large roasters, sprinkling with salt and pepper as you do so.

Spoon 5 cans of soup over each roaster. Don't dilute. Cover. Bake in 350ºF (180ºC) oven for about 2 hours until tender. Allow more time if chops not browned first. Serves 45 people, 2 chops each.

CROWDED CHICKEN

The quickest of any chicken to do ahead of time.

Chicken breasts and some thighs	32 lbs.	14.4 kg
Envelopes dry onion soup mix	14 — 1½ oz.	14 — 42.5 g

Cut breasts into 3 pieces each with cleaver or small hatchet. Layer in 2 turkey-sized roasters, skin side up. Cover each layer with onion soup mix using half the chicken and half the soup mix per roaster. Cover with foil. Bake in 350°F (180°C) oven for 2 hours. Test for doneness. Cover and continue to bake until fork tender in center of roaster second layer down. Serves 50.

METRIC CONVERSION

Throughout this book measurements are given in conventional and metric measure. To compensate for differences between the two measurements due to rounding, a full metric measure is not always used.
The cup used is the standard 8 fluid ounce.
Temperature is given in degrees Fahrenheit and Celsius.
Baking pan measurements are in inches and centimetres, as well as quarts and litres.
An exact conversion is given below as well as the working equivalent.

Spoons	Exact Conversion	Standard Metric Measure
¼ teaspoon	1.2 millilitres	1 mililitre
½ teaspoon	2.4 millilitres	2 millilitres
1 teaspoon	4.7 millilitres	5 millilitres
2 teaspoons	9.4 millilitres	10 millilitres
1 tablespoon	14.2 millilitres	15 millilitres

Cups		
¼ cup (4 T)	56.8 millilitres	50 millilitres
⅓ cup (5⅓ T)	75.6 millilitres	75 millilitres
½ cup (8 T)	113.7 millilitres	125 millilitres
⅔ cup (10⅔ T)	151.2 millilitres	150 millilitres
¾ cup (12 T)	170.5 millilitres	175 millilitres
1 cup (16 T)	227.3 millilitres	250 millilitres
4½ cups	984.8 millilitres	1000 millilitres, 1 litre

Ounces — Weight		
1 oz.	28.3 grams	30 grams
2 oz.	56.7 grams	55 grams
3 oz.	85 grams	85 grams
4 oz.	113.4 grams	125 grams
5 oz.	141.7 grams	140 grams
6 oz.	170.1 grams	170 grams
7 oz.	198.4 grams	200 grams
8 oz.	226.8 grams	250 grams
16 oz.	453.6 grams	500 grams
32 oz.	917.2 grams	1000 grams, 1 kg

Pans, Casseroles

8 × 8 inch, 20 × 20 cm, 2L	8 × 2 inch round, 20 × 5 cm, 2L
9 × 9 inch, 22 × 22 cm, 2.5L	9 × 2 inch round, 22 × 5 cm, 2.5L
9 × 13 inch, 22 × 33 cm, 4L	10 × 4½ inch tube, 25 × 11 cm, 5L
10 × 15 inch, 25 × 38 cm, 1.2L	8 × 4 × 3 inch loaf, 20 × 10 × 7 cm, 1.5L
11 × 17 inch, 28 × 43 cm, 1.5L	9 × 5 × 3 inch loaf, 23 × 12 × 7 cm, 2L

Oven Temperatures

Fahrenheit	Celsius	Fahrenheit	Celsius	Fahrenheit	Celsius
175°	80°	300°	150°	425°	220°
200°	100°	325°	160°	450°	230°
225°	110°	350°	180°	475°	240°
250°	120°	375°	190°	500°	260°
275°	140°	400°	200°		

(continued on next page)

151

(continued on next page)

(continued on next page)

(continued on next page)

Company's Coming — Taste The Tradition

SAVE $5.00

Mail to:
COMPANY'S COMING PUBLISHING LIMITED
BOX 8037, STATION "F"
EDMONTON, ALBERTA, CANADA T6H 4N9

Please send the following number of **Company's Coming Cookbooks** to the address on the reverse side of this coupon:

Qty.	Title	Each	Total
	150 DELICIOUS SQUARES	$9.95	
	CASSEROLES	$9.95	
	MUFFINS & MORE	$9.95	
	SALADS	$9.95	
	APPETIZERS	$9.95	
	DESSERTS	$9.95	
	SOUPS & SANDWICHES	$9.95	
	HOLIDAY ENTERTAINING	$9.95	
	COOKIES	$9.95	
	VEGETABLES	$9.95	
	MAIN COURSES	$9.95	
	PASTA (April 1990)	$9.95	
	JEAN PARÉ'S FAVORITES VOLUME ONE 232 pages, hard cover	$17.95	

Total Qty.		
	Total Cost of Cookbooks	$
	Plus $1.00 postage and handling per copy	$
Less $5.00 for every third copy per order		— $
Plus International Shipping Expenses (add $4.00 if outside Canada and U.S.A.)		$
Total Amount Enclosed		$

Special Mail Offer: Order any 2 **Company's Coming Cookbooks** by mail at regular prices and **save $5.00** on every third copy per order.
Not valid in combination with any other offer.

Orders Outside Canada — amount enclosed must be paid in U.S. Funds.

Make cheque or money order payable to: "Company's Coming Publishing Limited

Prices subject to change after December 31, 1992.

Sorry, no C.O.D.'s.

GIVE *Company's Coming* TO A FRIEND!

Please send Company's Coming Cookbooks listed on the reverse side of this coupon to:

NAME _____

STREET _____

CITY _____

PROVINCE/STATE _____ POSTAL CODE/ZIP _____

GIFT GIVING — WE MAKE IT EASY!

We will send Company's Coming cookbooks directly to the recipients of your choice — the perfect gift for birthdays, showers, Mother's Day, Father's Day, graduation or any occasion!

Please specify the number of copies of each title on the reverse side of this coupon and provide us with the name and address for each gift order. Enclose a personal note or card and we will include it with your order . . .

. . . and don't forget to take advantage of the **$5.00 saving** — buy 2 copies of **Company's Coming Cookbooks** by mail and **save $5.00** on every third copy per order.

Company's Coming — We Make It Easy — You Make it Delicious!

GIVE *Company's Coming* TO A FRIEND!

Please send Company's Coming Cookbooks listed on the reverse side of this coupon to:

NAME _____

STREET _____

CITY _____

PROVINCE/STATE _____ POSTAL CODE/ZIP _____

GIFT GIVING — WE MAKE IT EASY!

We will send Company's Coming cookbooks directly to the recipients of your choice — the perfect gift for birthdays, showers, Mother's Day, Father's Day, graduation or any occasion!

Please specify the number of copies of each title on the reverse side of this coupon and provide us with the name and address for each gift order. Enclose a personal note or card and we will include it with your order . . .

. . . and don't forget to take advantage of the **$5.00 saving** — buy 2 copies of **Company's Coming Cookbooks** by mail and **save $5.00** on every third copy per order.

Company's Coming — We Make It Easy — You Make it Delicious!

Company's Coming

Taste The Tradition

SAVE $5.00

Mail to:
COMPANY'S COMING PUBLISHING LIMITED
BOX 8037, STATION "F"
EDMONTON, ALBERTA, CANADA T6H 4N9

Please send the following number of **Company's Coming Cookbooks** to the address on the reverse side of this coupon:

Qty.	Title	Each	Total
	150 DELICIOUS SQUARES	$9.95	
	CASSEROLES	$9.95	
	MUFFINS & MORE	$9.95	
	SALADS	$9.95	
	APPETIZERS	$9.95	
	DESSERTS	$9.95	
	SOUPS & SANDWICHES	$9.95	
	HOLIDAY ENTERTAINING	$9.95	
	COOKIES	$9.95	
	VEGETABLES	$9.95	
	MAIN COURSES	$9.95	
	PASTA (April 1990)	$9.95	
	JEAN PARÉ'S FAVORITES VOLUME ONE 232 pages, hard cover	$17.95	

Total Qty.		
	Total Cost of Cookbooks	$
	Plus $1.00 postage and handling per copy	$
Less $5.00 for every third copy per order		— $
Plus International Shipping Expenses (add $4.00 if outside Canada and U.S.A.)		$
Total Amount Enclosed		$

Special Mail Offer: Order any 2 **Company's Coming Cookbooks** by mail at regular prices and **save $5.00** on every third copy per order.
Not valid in combination with any other offer.

Orders Outside Canada — amount enclosed must be paid in U.S. Funds.

Make cheque or money order payable to: "Company's Coming Publishing Limited

Prices subject to change after December 31, 1992.

Sorry, no C.O.D.'s.

Company's Coming

Taste The Tradition

SAVE $5.00

Mail to:
COMPANY'S COMING PUBLISHING LIMITED
BOX 8037, STATION "F"
EDMONTON, ALBERTA, CANADA T6H 4N9

Please send the following number of **Company's Coming Cookbooks** to the address on the reverse side of this coupon:

Qty.	Title	Each	Total
	150 DELICIOUS SQUARES	$9.95	
	CASSEROLES	$9.95	
	MUFFINS & MORE	$9.95	
	SALADS	$9.95	
	APPETIZERS	$9.95	
	DESSERTS	$9.95	
	SOUPS & SANDWICHES	$9.95	
	HOLIDAY ENTERTAINING	$9.95	
	COOKIES	$9.95	
	VEGETABLES	$9.95	
	MAIN COURSES	$9.95	
	PASTA (April 1990)	$9.95	
	JEAN PARÉ'S FAVORITES VOLUME ONE 232 pages, hard cover	$17.95	

Total Qty.		
	Total Cost of Cookbooks	$
	Plus $1.00 postage and handling per copy	$
Less $5.00 for every third copy per order		— $
Plus International Shipping Expenses (add $4.00 if outside Canada and U.S.A.)		$
Total Amount Enclosed		$

Special Mail Offer: Order any 2 **Company's Coming Cookbooks** by mail at regular prices and **save $5.00** on every third copy per order.
Not valid in combination with any other offer.

Orders Outside Canada — amount enclosed must be paid in U.S. Funds.

Make cheque or money order payable to: "Company's Coming Publishing Limited

Prices subject to change after December 31, 1992.

Sorry, no C.O.D.'s.

GIVE *Company's Coming* TO A FRIEND!

Please send Company's Coming Cookbooks listed on the reverse side of this coupon to:

NAME _____

STREET _____

CITY _____

PROVINCE/STATE _____ POSTAL CODE/ZIP _____

GIFT GIVING — WE MAKE IT EASY!

We will send Company's Coming cookbooks directly to the recipients of your choice — the perfect gift for birthdays, showers, Mother's Day, Father's Day, graduation or any occasion!

Please specify the number of copies of each title on the reverse side of this coupon and provide us with the name and address for each gift order. Enclose a personal note or card and we will include it with your order . . .

. . . and don't forget to take advantage of the **$5.00 saving** — buy 2 copies of **Company's Coming Cookbooks** by mail and **save $5.00** on every third copy per order.

Company's Coming — We Make It Easy — You Make it Delicious!

GIVE *Company's Coming* TO A FRIEND!

Please send Company's Coming Cookbooks listed on the reverse side of this coupon to:

NAME _____

STREET _____

CITY _____

PROVINCE/STATE _____ POSTAL CODE/ZIP _____

GIFT GIVING — WE MAKE IT EASY!

We will send Company's Coming cookbooks directly to the recipients of your choice — the perfect gift for birthdays, showers, Mother's Day, Father's Day, graduation or any occasion!

Please specify the number of copies of each title on the reverse side of this coupon and provide us with the name and address for each gift order. Enclose a personal note or card and we will include it with your order . . .

. . . and don't forget to take advantage of the **$5.00 saving** — buy 2 copies of **Company's Coming Cookbooks** by mail and **save $5.00** on every third copy per order.

Company's Coming — We Make It Easy — You Make it Delicious!